Amanda Reynal

DESIGNING ROOMS with JOIE DE VIVRE

a fresh take on classic style

Foreword by Stephen Orr, editor in chief
Better Homes & Gardens

Abrams, New York

To my mother, Nancy, who is the personification of joie de vivre.

She spreads joy to all she encounters and is effortlessly chic in all realms of style. She is an inimitable human whom I am privileged to call Mom. I have become who I am thanks to a lifetime of her gracious and impeccable influence and have learned the importance of aesthetics from her. From breathtaking gardens and historic homes to the myriad art museums she has shared with me, she has always encouraged me to see the beauty in each detail that surrounds us.

Contents

8 FOREWORD BY STEPHEN ORR

11 *chapter 1*
DESIGN FUNDAMENTALS

43 *chapter 2*
COLORING OUTSIDE THE LINES

73 *chapter 3*
CREATING WOW MOMENTS:
PUSHING THE ENVELOPE

107 *chapter 4*
LAYERING AND THE
DETAILS THAT MAKE
AN IMPRESSION

145 *chapter 5*
UPDATING CLASSICS:
DECORATIVE TOUCHES THAT
ARE NOW AND FOREVER

179 *chapter 6*
TURNING PRACTICAL INTO
STUNNING

213 *chapter 7*
JOYFUL ROOMS

253 ACKNOWLEDGMENTS
255 ABOUT THE AUTHOR

Foreword

I first admired Amanda Reynal's interior design at her home in Des Moines, Iowa. I was new in town as the editor of *Better Homes & Gardens.* Amanda and her husband, Mike, both of whom were also transplanted East Coasters, had kindly invited me over. Their home, just a block away from mine at the time, was a gracious 1910 center-hall stucco house. On entering, I was immediately struck by Amanda's talent, first by her attention to surfaces and the color and pattern in her work. As I looked more closely, I noticed how completely she transforms a space through a studied and informed sense of historical layering. Amanda knows the history of interior design—and it shows.

As an editor who has made my living over the past decades publishing other people's houses and gardens, I have reviewed thousands of scouting shots. Sometimes a person will ask me, What are you looking for in order to approve a story? The answer is simple: I'm looking for a point of view. I'm not trying to judge how other people live their lives and what it takes to make them comfortable and happy; I'm looking for originality—an eye—that will spark the interest of the reader and give them ideas and inspiration. I remember the dining room in that house in Des Moines (the Reynals have since moved on to another house a few blocks away)—its ceiling, covered in marbleized Florentine paper from Schumacher, and updated traditional style that made guests, who were already wrapped in the warm candlelight of Amanda's table, feel like they were nestled inside a giant lacquered jewel box. Amanda's version of good design isn't meant to impress or intimidate; it's meant to make herself, her family, and her

guests feel joy—happy to finally get home, happy to reunite, happy to be invited over.

The next house I visited that Amanda designed was a collaboration of an unusual kind. In a mountain hamlet in Upstate New York that is known for being a historic creative community, the Reynals have a house that was once the home of the first female interior designer in the country, Candace Thurber Wheeler. In this nineteenth-century house so rich with heritage and provenance, Amanda, because of her historical knowledge, knew what to augment, what to modernize, and what to leave alone. I remember admiring the library with an original Arts and Crafts frieze painted by Wheeler's daughter, depicting a field of golden lilies. Other parts of the house had been modernized with splashes of Amanda's signature bold color mix, which sometimes references the preppy parts of Connecticut or the more social parts of Palm Beach, Florida. Everywhere, the past and the present were blended with one woman's decorative layer, feathered and updated by another, generations removed from the original but full of respect and admiration.

The most recent of Amanda's homes that I've visited is also in Des Moines; unlike her first place, this one is farmhouse-style, an updated 1970s suburban two-story house that was a white box of a dry-walled interior. When she showed me the Realtor photographs, I was surprised she wanted to decorate a place with such blank slate. But like any good interior designer, Amanda clearly had a vision of what she could do with it. When I came for dinner after she had been there only a few months, I was shocked. Where boring walls once existed, Amanda created an enveloping cocoon of textures and colors. Golden, glowing grass cloth cloaked the walls of a family room set off by dramatic black lacquer woven wall covering and bold accents. Amanda's interiors are always done. No corner, not even a utility room, is left unconsidered. Each room is like a visual mood board come to life. You can almost imagine her pin-up mood board of textural elements, patterns, swatches, trim, and paint colors when you walk in. Amanda's method is based on curiosity and learning, both from life experience and books, but also from just being smart and keeping her eyes open. Mix that with an innate sense of the lifestyle she wants to enjoy and telegraph—it's one that comes from experience, not just from browsing Pinterest.

As someone who has a hard time imagining where to start when confronted with a blank room, I admire interior designers for knowing even where to begin. Sussing out how to find that first spark of a color scheme. How to add the layering that takes a flat white space from the default to the divine. Most importantly, knowing how to stop. Part of having an educated eye is realizing when to step away from what you're building and knowing that that previous dollop of style was all that was needed.

With this book, Amanda's first, I hope that she realizes that this is an important record of her career only this far. We look forward to many more projects and books in her future. If Amanda is anything like Candace Wheeler, who lived to be ninety-six, there will be many years of eye-catching colors, patterns, and layering to come.

—Stephen Orr, editor in chief,
Better Homes & Gardens

Cloth

chapter 1

DESIGN FUNDAMENTALS

I believe that you have to know the rules to break the rules. In my work as an interior designer, I am known for confident color choices and eye-catching rooms. I love to incorporate arresting prints, intriguing silhouettes, richly patterned fabrics, and intricate wallpaper. A well-designed and often dramatic ceiling has become one of my signatures. However, while I love all these wow design moments, there is an art to how I design a space that involves an unexpected mix of classic and cool, sophisticated and playful, and pizzazz with serene. It's all about balance.

In this age of Instagram and Pinterest, bold design moves are rewarded. Beige and gray alone simply don't have the same showstopping quality. Statement-making design has never been more popular, and to pull it off successfully requires an intentional process. Without an understanding of the core rules of design, it is easy to overdo it, become stuck while chasing trends, and invest in decorating features that are labeled "dated" sooner than later.

Where to start? Fundamentally, design begins and ends with emotions. When we are at home, we have ideas and wants regarding how the spaces should make us feel: joyful when we are surrounded by our dearest; inspired when we are dreaming about what's next; and comforted during those times when we want to feel at peace and seek refuge.

After examining the feeling our home evokes in its existing condition and identifying what we *hope* for it to become, we can then launch the decorative process. Let's break down the various elements such as texture, color, form, and lighting, and then ask ourselves questions about preferences and the desired end result. Do we tend toward a robust, collected scheme

or one that is pared down and edited? These are the decisions that will craft the style of a home. The good news about design is that, with so many of its arms and categories, the lines between what's right or wrong are blurred. The success of a design is oftentimes led by personal preference, and usually that can be enough to create a beautiful environment. There are plenty of instances, however, when I adopt a process that facilitates the design and selections in a more methodical way. That's what this chapter is all about—sharing the fundamentals of design that require attention during the process and the information that will make the decision-making an inspired and well-informed experience. As you read this book, I hope you'll find my theories, methods, and approach instructive and helpful as you plan for inspired beauty in your own home. Your connection with a design is what will make it resonate with you. Our homes ideally reflect not just

function, but an assortment of many things that we love. To achieve this, it's essential that each detail be considered. Being thoughtful about all elements, whether grand or basic, from the switch plate covers and moldings to an antique piece of furniture that may benefit from a facelift, is all important. This acknowledgment of all aspects of the design, whether large or small, is what gives our spaces authenticity and makes them personal.

The best results come from an energetic and tireless design process with time spent on the overall mood of the space as well on as the details that make it yours. After completing myriad projects for others over the years and designing for myself, too, I understand that it would be tempting to throw in the towel instead of focusing on every detail. However, when I am designing a home, *every* element is critical, from hard surfaces, to hardware, to bath towels. From selecting a sculptural and handsome faucet to styling the

Brown furniture is one hallmark of traditional style.
When you appoint it to a room, make it come alive with
a bevy of patterns that suggest an active environment.

accessories collection on a case of shelves, each aspect of the decision process contributes to the overall scheme.

I'm a lifelong embroidery enthusiast and love to personalize through monograms, so I look for opportunities to produce them. Just another plain towel in the bathroom would be a missed chance for an elegant detail such as an embroidered dahlia, a framed monogram, or a charming toy stitched to mark the holidays. Monograms can be used on linens and stationery, too.

If some aspects of design feel arduous, then take them one element at a time. We take pride in our homes, and so spending the time to hone design particulars that we adore is worth it. Like a tailored blazer that completes our look, design should be thoughtful and buttoned-up, too.

IDENTIFYING STYLE

Before you confirm that you prefer one style or another, it's important to understand how the different styles reveal themselves. After all, design is subjective, so what one person might consider to be modern could in fact be traditional, simply because of its tenure in history. I want to share my style definitions with you. They are how my team and I communicate as we tackle each project.

Traditional

Traditional, as it applies to design, immediately makes me think of history and stamps of approval, because the components of this category make regular comebacks. Traditional harkens back to styles and details that have existed for many years. It is largely based on eighteenth- and nineteenth-century European and American architecture and furniture. When I define it, I'm looking at specific classic details and applications that feel current but are also a nod to the past. I'm also thinking about whether a detail feels correct and appropriate in the interior, regardless of the period it originated.

ABOVE *For day-to-day life, a classic dining room exudes beauty without a lot of adornments. I look forward to those moments, however, when I entertain and can dress the table with extra flair.*

OPPOSITE *When you start with a foundation of classic elements, design can make a shift to natural colors with ease.*

It's important to acknowledge that traditional interiors can be viewed in two ways: aesthetics and time. I'll start with the aesthetics of traditional style. We tend to label as "traditional" looks that include brown period furniture such as Queen Anne and Chippendale, or prints with dainty country roses, or wool plaids. However, traditional can encompass modernized applications of a detail. Adding passementerie to pillows or drapery treatments; accessorizing with blue-and-white porcelain; wrapping a room in a chinoiserie mural all qualify as traditional, even if what you are seeing is a modern version of the detail.

Time is on the side of traditional, too, and sometimes that means embracing looks that at first glance might be considered modern. Let's examine the creations of Eero Saarinen, Ludwig Mies van der Rohe, Ray and Charles Eames, and other iconic modern classic legends. If you are reading this book, then I'll bet that you've stumbled upon the sleek Barcelona chair or daybed once or twice, probably in buttery black leather. At the time it was created in 1929, its biscuit tufting was a modern update to the fussier, more dramatic tufting of English Victorian seating. Tantalizing interiors for almost a century, the Barcelona chair has become a quiet but dynamic juxtaposition to curvy wood pieces. Albeit younger, with a 1956 birthdate, Saarinen's graceful tulip table has delivered just as much sculpture as it has function.

Traditional style is the careful curation of many periods. Its roots are in the past but it promises beauty indefinitely.

Timeless and Classic

You may agree that timeless style always looks appropriate, because it can fit within different periods of architecture. Something that is timeless can live quietly among the curves, rich wood tones, feminine florals, and handsome plaids of all things traditional. Likewise, timeless style can add an inviting warmth to the sleekness that trumpets the modern look.

First, I'd like to address specific design details that I consider to be timeless. White-painted woodwork, for instance, has always seemed to work. Moldings, millwork, and thick and soaring staircases with weighty details are what people covet as they are looking at existing architecture or planning to build something new. White woodwork looks good with an assembly of textured fabrics or with the contrast of brown wood furniture, but adds a level of comfort to modern pieces, too. Architecturally, it's threaded throughout many different eras. Decoratively, it embraces and enhances everything that is placed within its shell.

Animal prints have taken us through the last century and are now considered timeless. I tend to use animal prints in design the same way that I do in fashion, as an accent, not as the main event. In an interior, I would assign a medium-scaled animal print pattern to something secondary such as a pair of stools that live under a console table or a pair of ottomans, to add kick to an otherwise solid-colored seating environment.

Natural fibers also fall into the "timeless" bucket. I love a pair of velvet slippers or a velvet blazer to wear with jeans. The same is true in an interior. Velvet doesn't have to be shiny and fancy. I prefer a velvet that wears well with age, like a linen or cotton version. A velvet sofa is both chic and very comfortable. Velvet doesn't have to take over a room. Just one piece that can take on a different feeling when you are ready for a changeup will suffice.

Classics can be on-trend without being trendy. The best part is that if classics wane in popularity, they will still mingle beautifully in your home, even if moved to a new location.

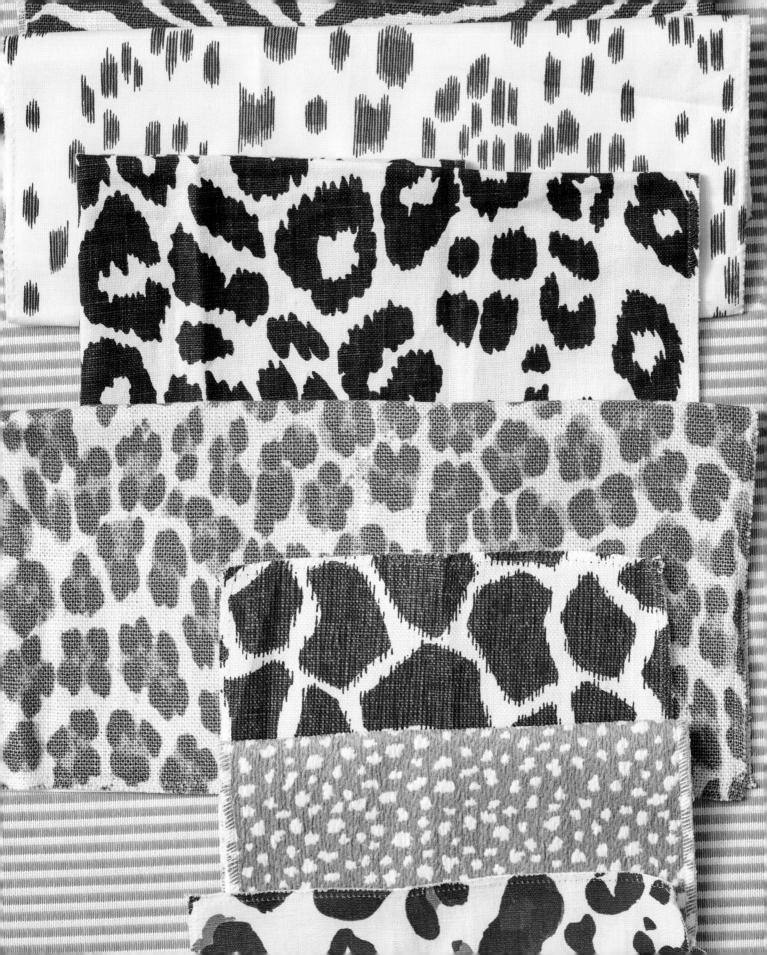

ABOVE *An otherwise neutral space only requires one strong element to take it out of a quiet existence. Here, a painted red floor energizes the scheme.*

LEFT *A balanced room requires an understanding of scale, proportion, and editing. Solid colors were chosen for velvet armchairs so they wouldn't compete with the pattern of the rug.*

A blend of solid colors, neutrals, and
natural elements make a dining room fresh
and modern.

Linens and cottons exist that are not heavy and are ideal for curtain panels when you beckon in natural light, or duvet covers when you don't want to add physical weight to the bed. Classic motifs such as checks, plaids, stripes, and chevrons always have a version that is up-to-date. The same is true for more complex prints such as a tree-of-life pattern.

It's common for us to use the terms *timeless* and *classic* interchangeably. I think they are, to a degree. Timeless to me is the overarching theme. Classic falls within that category.

Classics can be on-trend without being trendy. The best part is that if classics wane in popularity, they will still mingle beautifully in your home, even if moved to a new location. With a little imagination, creativity, and an open mind, a classic is *always* right.

Modern

Modern style perhaps requires the most clarification, because in the world of design it's common to use the term incorrectly. Modern style is rooted in a specific moment in time. The modernist period of art and architecture started being noticed early in the twentieth century. At that time, there was so much that was new. The newness wasn't solely from minimalist architecture and forms that tended to be sleek and uncluttered, with little if any embellishment. It also embraced new materials including plate glass, steel, and, notably, plastic. The period brought in a renaissance in design and lifestyle, and it was classified as modern, because at the time it was. With modern architecture preceding them, modern interiors exploded in the 1950s and 1960s. Television was still in its early days, but pop culture brought modern aesthetics to living rooms through the screen, where we came to love the interiors and the families who lived in them. On *I Love Lucy*, Lucy regularly lobbied for Ricky to allow an apartment redo with new furniture. To Ricky's dismay, she landed a mid-century modern suite as the result of a Lucy antic gone wrong.

The word *modern* is sometimes mistakenly used when what we really mean is *contemporary*. In design, *contemporary* means anything that is new, whether it is classic, trendy, clean-lined, or decorative. It refers to the present and is the opposite of antique. Contemporary style oftentimes incorporates elements of modern style, but it doesn't adhere to that only. When I think about contemporary, I tend to land on solid colors, neutrals, abstract art, geometrics, and natural elements brought together in creative ways. Contemporary is more about innovation and is less inspired by the past.

A GUIDE TO STYLE THROUGH PATTERNS

Having so many decorative options means it's difficult to give a blueprint for exact results. When it comes to patterns, though, I have some easy tips that will assist you in hitting the mark for specific styles.

- If you want pretty, choose a pattern with movement.
- If you want daring, try a bold geometric.
- If you are looking for warmth, choose textiles or other materials with inherent pattern or soft and woven textures.
- If you want something tailored and masculine, lean on the look of men's suiting materials.

When I'm making selections for myself, I'll get excited about a particular fabric that I've been drawn to since the first time that I saw it, or to the shape of a beautiful lamp. What really makes me beam, however, is seeing all the components come together in the end. That's why I'm encouraging you to pay close attention and try not to settle for something that you don't find attractive, comfortable, useful, or necessary. I understand that limited financial resources can quickly crush some design aspirations. I've been there myself and find it important to have a balance of high- and low-priced design elements to complete my look.

Barstools can be sculptural additions to a kitchen. The classic silhouette of these barstools suggests lounging for a comfortable stay, much like fully upholstered seating in a living room.

The Evolution of Organic

Organic was once centered around materials: raw wood, scratchy jute, and anything else that came from nature and was left in a somewhat unaltered form. Additionally, we embraced the maker movement, which highlighted artisans who produced small batches of their works, from ceramics to textiles, oftentimes with flowing lines that didn't support symmetry. Makers have recognized that designs past represent so much beauty that can be reinterpreted. Revisiting the original way of fabricating goods to produce a personalized product allows the recipient a connection with the artisan and the opportunity for a look that is traditional and artisanal at the same time.

A pair of lamps is a fundamental design tool that provides balance, symmetry, and a sense of order. This pair shows off a modernized, abstract glaze.

FLOOR PLANS

The main goal of creating a plan is to ensure that the space functions and that all the furniture fits well.

If you find floor plans challenging, here's my advice: Lean on symmetry. In a living room, for instance, it's common to see a sofa facing a pair of chairs in front of a fireplace with a cocktail table in the middle. There's nothing that is new or creative about this arrangement, but it's balanced and it works, and function is key. There's a reason it works to situate bedside tables and lamps on each side of the bed. Similarly, it makes sense to place a sideboard or credenza a close distance from a dining table. Remember that when it comes to furniture plans, it's fine to repeat what you've been looking at for decades when it works with the scale and function of the room. Use symmetry and balance as your guides.

REMODEL, REDECORATE, OR A BIT OF BOTH (LITTLE OF EACH)?

Homeowners tend to look at architecture as a two-options-only decision. Does the project warrant a full renovation that includes gutting the house? Or would a decorative facelift be enough?

The good news is that there are in fact more than two options. If the project needs it and the budget supports it, a full renovation can be an excellent choice. You can focus solely on decorative elements if the architecture and function of the home are already working. You also have the option of doing something that's a little bit in between. I'll address that idea first.

Think about what architectural details could do for your living space if none exist now. Add interior architecture such as crown molding in a room that doesn't have any. A simple staircase might graduate to a starring role with a layer of paneling applied to its side. If your ceiling height is elevated or you want it to appear to be more interesting, a coffered treatment could make a statement overhead. Instead of a full bathroom redo, you could replace the vanity, which, if it has any age to it, likely wants a new cabinet style.

The classic shapes of a pair of sofas balance the handsome dark tone of the wall. Matching armchairs with a pattern that mixes both neutrals with gold in a medium value bridge the two.

Sometimes a remodel isn't necessary. Before ripping out original materials, conduct a little research to find out if the materials can be updated. For instance, an old bathroom floor might have beautiful old tile that looks filthy and tired. Ask around to see what it would take to have the tile restored. Most people take the easy route and start pulling up original materials because they think that *dirty* means *dated*. Keep in mind that replacing the tile could be more costly, and you might not be able to match the quality of the original. The same is true with solid-core doors. What is the cost of doors of a similar quality? Dingy brown doors that are sanded and stained a chic black finish just might hit the on-trend, contemporary mark that you are aiming for. Furthermore, restoring an old material like tile or wood can maintain the integrity of an old house. Mimicking the character of an old home with new materials that are void of patina and age can be difficult, plus that usually would be very costly.

I have one additional bit of information to share regarding the use of original materials: They are eco-friendly. While an impressive amount of attention has been devoted to developing materials that are environmentally responsible, one way that guarantees a zero carbon footprint is to use components that already exist.

In the end, before deciding which size project to embark on, consider if you are adding value to your home, if the timing is right to do a big project, or if a smaller one feels more manageable.

SCALE

Often, when I visit someone's home, I see a common mistake that can easily be avoided: elements that are too small or too large for the room. Pieces of the wrong size can misdirect the eye. Scale shares the same level as color when it comes to intimidating design factors. People routinely believe that a piece won't fit if it is big. The reality is, however, that buying large pieces can fill a room nicely, decreasing the number that are needed. Bits and pieces of small things don't

ABOVE *Black and white is not harsh when softened by a third color like the pale yellow here. The sunny hue weaves its way into a plaid on chair upholstery, cushions on the banquette, and trim on the drapery panels.*

OPPOSITE *Layering is a fundamental of a successful interior, blending materials, colors, and forms to create a cohesive look.*

The blue glaze of shapely matching lamps anchors the varied visual textures of the wallpaper, credenza, artwork, and floor.

read well and can appear cluttered. However, if furniture is oversized and bulky, it runs the risk of looking overwhelming and unrefined.

Choosing the proper scale for a room's elements is critical to a successful design. First, take a look at the architecture. Consider the ceiling height, dimensions of the room, and what you want to convey. For instance, a room with a high ceiling will likely require pieces with heft to anchor the environment. A three-seater sofa might be an ideal piece to ground the space and carry the room's volume. On the other hand, a small, intimate apartment would be better off with furniture of a smaller scale. A settee or love seat might be a good option for a space that likely will never have to accommodate many guests. If you have a small room that you are furnishing, you might forgo a bunch of chairs for a sectional that hugs the walls. Also, who says that a sofa is required? Think about a group of four armchairs, which might be ideal if you have only a few people over to visit at a time. This arrangement ensures easy and inclusive conversation.

When it comes to accessories, play with scale a bit to see what delivers a dramatic look for you. For example, plunge into the category of oversized lamps for an entry foyer console table vignette that wows. Small slipper chairs always add an extra dose of elegance without an intrusive profile. And when you don't have large-scale accessories, create volume with a collection of similar objects of the same color. Styling methods aren't solely about polishing a space. They offer solutions, too.

The scale of patterns can also alter a room. Whether you are serious about a pattern or not, I'll bet those dynamic, oversized wallpaper patterns grab your attention.

Before selecting colors, textures, or choosing specific pieces of furniture, focus on scale. Measure, then measure again, for results that launch your design on a positive note.

BALANCE

I've already praised the effectiveness of symmetry. We tend to prioritize symmetry because it feels good. It's calming and doesn't cause confusion. Where there is symmetry, however, it's important to throw a curveball here and there so the scheme doesn't look too contrived. For instance, in a living room that reads "polite," with solid colors and tailored furniture, you might add a vintage, oddly shaped side table with an unexpected finish. Not only will a piece like this bring personality and decorative charm to the space, it will be sculptural. Also think about an asymmetrical piece of furniture. A sofa with an organic, curvy, asymmetrical back might be enough of a modern kick to offset the traditional underpinnings of an old house. Likewise, an asymmetrical light fixture might throw a bit of much-needed imperfection into an otherwise balanced room.

Distribute color schemes with a mix of solids, prints, and woven fabrics. Be careful, though, that the fabrics you choose complement and don't compete with each other.

In the end, remember that part of balance is *imbalance*. It's the addition of subtle nuances that will throw the foundation in an intriguing direction. Balance is about contrast.

RIGHT Playful notes are welcome in an environment of light neutral tones. The cheerful palette of this rug lends bold tones that don't overwhelm.

Thoughts on Rugs

Rugs are important, because they oftentimes direct a room's design scheme. When my team is selecting rugs for our projects, we adhere to a general rule of thumb that I always find helpful: Pick a rug that takes up the majority of the floor space and leaves a 6-inch to 12-inch border. If you are drawn to patterned rugs, don't hesitate to choose the rug first and then build the rest of the room around its palette and scale. It can be an oversized Persian, Oushak, or large-scale geometric carpet. The rug should be large enough for all furniture to sit on top of it. If there is already a significant amount of pattern and movement elsewhere in a room, a simple rug might be your best bet. I tend toward a natural fiber for a rug, such as wool, abaca, or sisal. Also, keep in mind that not every rug must be similar in quality. Invest in a rug to go where you will enjoy it as you would a piece of art. Choose something simple that's intended for indoor-outdoor use to withstand areas with high amounts of traffic.

ACQUIRING AND EDITING

For the occasions that you are out and about shopping design emporiums, antiques vendors, and flea markets, I would like to offer the following advice: Think of retail design sources as a *gallery* of goods, the way you think of artwork in a gallery. When you visit an art museum, for example, you probably leisurely stroll from one gallery to the next, seeking out those special pieces that move you. Never would you think of hauling every piece of artwork home, even if the security detail allowed it. Consider retail goods in the same manner. But if you are serious about bringing them home, imagine where they will go and measure the space you have at home and then the actual pieces before you pull out your credit card.

Think about how an object will mingle with the other elements that will be around it.

Also keep seasonality in mind. The daylight and colors will both eventually change, so think about how a piece might look in the brightness of white snow or against the backdrop of chartreuse in the spring as trees are budding.

Layering furniture and accessories can take time, so have patience and persevere.

The Art of the Edit

Sometimes it's fun to subscribe to the more-is-more approach. Maximalism, however, can be overwhelming when individual objects aren't supported by breathing room and therefore drown in visual noise. A situation like this requires editing so that each piece can be enjoyed.

When outfitting a room, here's my advice: You can have everything, but not all at once. Rotate your collections and objects and acknowledge that it's OK to store things for a while to give them a rest. If you are like me, you'll forget

Stylish accents keep balanced palettes from becoming boring. Here, two stools covered in a leopard print give a punchy kick to a green-and-ivory living room.

that you had a piece, and when it resurfaces, you will delight in it all over again. For instance, a beautiful box on a coffee table that you picked up on a trip can move to another room. After all, it's just a box. The same is true for most accessories. Don't hesitate to move them around the house or eliminate them completely. Even in my

Rotate your collections and objects and acknowledge that it's OK to store things for a while to give them a rest.

own home, I can become blind to the way certain objects are layered and styled. I try to look at my rooms through a fresh pair of eyes. My routine is to address this after a trip that has taken me away from my home for some time. It's easier to spot these rearranging opportunities when you are not surrounded by the objects every day.

That's what makes design special and personal: a process that supports ideas of one thing leading to another. It's intertwined, woven together, and always has the capability of reaching beauty.

Once you have your furniture plan laid out and major pieces are selected, think about those ancillary pieces that might introduce a personal touch. Furniture such as your sofa or bed might be timeless and you may very well love them, but it's the small forms that imbue interest. Search for a vintage bar cart or, for an updated look, consider my approach to a bar: I set it up on a credenza or chest of drawers instead. Having little drinks tables on hand makes sure that everyone has a safe and secure spot for their beverage.

SETTING THE DESIGN FOUNDATION

Architecture

I've already addressed architectural details. There are a couple of instances, however, where building moments can draw extra impact.

OPPOSITE *Simplicity is a design ally. Use it for moments of visual relief.*

I'm a big fan of built-in furniture. Who isn't? It provides architectural detail while offering integral storage and display areas. A built-in can be constructed as a unit with open shelving or drawers and a door if it will house materials that need to be disguised. These units allow us to use our spaces more efficiently, and my theory is, an efficient home is a happy one. Built-ins are one area of design that never seem to come with regrets. Think about where you might need extra storage or a place to showcase a collection. A built-in can be a cost-effective answer, especially if you choose a wood such as poplar, which can be finished with paint.

Fireplaces offer a similar level of joy. They evoke emotion, comfort, and warmth. Look at your mantel and evaluate if it's aligned with your architectural voice and design sensibilities. It might need a replacement with a new or found mantel that suits your style.

Anchor Pieces

There are certain furnishings in every home—necessary pieces that are essential to specific rooms. They are a constant and usually of an imposing size, making them challenging to move.

• **Dining tables.** Consider the shape and size of your dining room. How many people do you want to seat? Do you prefer small, intimate dinners for eight or fewer, or do you count the days until your extended family rings the doorbell for Thanksgiving dinner?

• **Beds.** I always lean toward comfort. For me, that means an upholstered headboard, because then I can comfortably prop up against it while reading or watching TV. Don't you want to invest in a bed that you cannot wait to crawl into every night?

Regardless of the activity in the space, fundamentals are the key to design success. Before you turn your focus to what's pretty and exciting, take the time to address the foundations of design. Once you have them established and settled, building an attractive environment will be joyful.

Buying in Pairs: When Two or Three Are Better Than One

Sometimes one just isn't enough, and an object needs a friend or, in this case, a twin. When you are making selections, you might consider the impact that a pair of an element will make versus a singular form. Ottomans, stools, lamps, throw pillows, and antiques are a good place to start with pairs. Pairs of furniture add another layer and oftentimes more seating. Pairs of accessories deliver balance. When it comes to artwork, a pair (or more) of works may offer better dimensions and proportions than a single big piece. If your room needs a moment of life, you might visit your local nursery for a pair of fig trees. An odd number of small wares such as decanters, creamware bowls, candlesticks, and picture frames with family photos all emphasize a form and give structure to the surface on which they are placed. Cluster photo frames, decanters, and candlesticks in groups of three to add interest and tension.

ABOVE *The navy blue built-ins in a traditional library create symmetry and a shell to add books and other treasures, and highlight an abstract piece of art.*

OPPOSITE *Finding a way to punctuate a solid-colored room is rather simple. Throw it a curveball of a texture, an oversized pattern, or bright green glassware showing through clear cabinet doors.*

chapter 2

COLORING
OUTSIDE THE LINES

e refer to a dynamic and vibrant life as a colorful one, because color is what makes life interesting. It's all around us and, whether it's intense or subdued, it sends a message and creates a mood.

Color can be soothing when we need a moment of rest. It can be bold and full of life when celebration calls. It can elevate the warmth that already comes from a houseful of guests on the holidays.

Your home *wants* color. Good news: The real-life definition of what color means varies. In this chapter I will take you through possibilities so you can commit your surroundings with confidence to a color scheme that's personal to you, or to something basic that uses color in small but impactful doses.

With an open mind to the inspirations that are all around you, you can allow color to saturate your home with interest and personality in various ways. Isn't that what living is all about?

INFORMED BY COLOR

When you think about it, there's nothing more instinctive, in a design sense, than color. After all, we can't turn our eyes on to only see our own aesthetic preferences. We can't help but be exposed to it all. Open the doors on a picture-perfect day, for instance. You immediately see the azure blue of the sky, and who wouldn't want to? In the same way, when you are out for a drive, you can't avoid a red stop sign or the blazing orange signage that alerts you to a dangerous area. Glowing neon lights at the entrance of a building, the bevy of daffodils

LEFT *Spring delivers
cheerful inspiration in
light and bright hues.*

OPPOSITE *Big statements
oftentimes can come
in small doses. In spots
where a touch of color
is needed, try a piece
of artwork before
committing to new paint
colors and wallpaper.*

or mums that seemingly landscapes every bank that you pass, and at other times the browns and grays of bare trees and dormant ground that is awaiting spring's arrival—they are all colorful moments that greet us while we are out and about. Some colors are ones that we label "beautiful," and others might seem like nothing that we'd ever want to invite into our homes.

That's where creativity enters in a way that can be powerful and meaningful. When we open our minds to taking a color that may not capture our fondness and make it beautiful, dynamic design happens. Any color can be seen as beautiful—it's all about how you use it.

To examine what colors are standouts to you, let's look at some key aesthetic parts of your life.

Take a Look at Where You Live Now

How would you describe your home as it exists? Does it quietly blend calming neutrals, or is its intention to dazzle with fun bolds and brights?

Our aesthetics evolve, and what we might be attracted to in one decade can be tired, dated, or been there, done that in the next. One approach that I use and could be useful to you is to review each element in each space to determine those components that you like best, and the ones that you can leave behind.

For example, I'm an art collector. I always have been passionate about art and can't imagine a time in my life when I won't find joy in my various works. But how and where they are displayed and hung might look a little different from one house to another. I'm not shy when it comes to layers. I have no problem building on a patterned wallpaper with a textural painting. If you usually find yourself hanging art on plain white walls, here's what I would do: Add some color to the background wall behind it. It doesn't have to be a heavily patterned wallcovering, just a splash of vibrancy that will give the artwork additional prominence.

Whether you have an art collection that you would never part with, or have been using a color that's a longtime favorite, looking at your home's design piece by piece helps you determine what you want to live with next. Your assessment as it applies to color can be used to enhance a piece that has perhaps existed in the background for too long.

Look Inside Your Closet

If there's one part of our style that can change with the wind, it's our wardrobe. Some of us like to wear neutrals, with color added only by accessories such as a vibrant scarf, a bright handbag, or a pair of shoes. Think about a basic but always in style outfit of denim jeans paired with a crisp white shirt. Those who adhere to a classic look may opt for gold hoop earrings and a warm brown camel-colored handbag. Personally, I would add a pop of color—strong color. I'm fairly committed to a couple of favorite gold necklaces that are special to me, but I may tie a colorful silk scarf around a handbag handle or wear a pair of hot

Review each element in each space to determine those components that you like best, and the ones that you can leave behind.

pink ballet flats. Chances are, my handbag or tote is a non-neutral color, too.

It's common knowledge that our wardrobes are indicative of how we want to live. It's what we feel good in and what is comfortable. Think about a low-key winter weekend, the kind that calls for a bottomless pot of coffee and a roster of must-see movies and must-read books. In that case, you'll find me in leggings and an oversized shaker knit sweater with my fuzzy shearling-lined slippers. You can bet that an extra-thick blanket will be wrapped around me, too.

If your affection for fashion rivals your fondness for interiors, use your daily wardrobe picks to play with colors. You'll quickly learn what works and what doesn't.

Inspiration is steps away out the front door. A fern frond was the springboard for a scheme that used a printed fern wallcovering and woody case goods.

A mood board is a good indicator of how colors will balance throughout a room. While I'm not one to use a lot of black, I wanted a fair amount in my living room. Playing with the black-toned fabrics gave me a sense of what I would be living with. Exchanging one black fabric for a lighter one would alter the balance.

ABOVE *There's something about a soothing palette in a bedroom that encourages quality downtime. Add a happy moment that boosts the cheer quotient without taking over the space.*

OPPOSITE *A painted piece of furniture is a go-to when a room needs to elevate its color attitude. In pale blue, this chest of drawers highlights the blue of the drapery fabric without being overpowering.*

Blue-and-white's familiar scheme is ideal for outdoor spaces. Use it on simple cushions, or try a ceramic stool to usher in the color duo.

Look Through Your Travel Photos

When you are planning to step away from your home, those places that get you most jazzed are also the places that can inform your design preferences. I, for instance, spend a lot of time in Florida. I find energy in the bright white and bright colors that are suitable for a sunshine-charged location.

The point is: We naturally gravitate over and over to places and things that we love. That's not to say that we don't occasionally go astray toward an outlier. Generally speaking, though, repetition is a telling indicator of what brings us visual joy. As you think about the colors that you want to live with next, examine the parts of your life that seemingly have nothing to do with design, because in the end, they always do.

DEVELOPING A PALETTE

When it comes to putting together a color scheme, I have one pivotal piece of advice: Keep your eyes open and take note of everything.

As a designer, I've always taken an academic approach when it comes to color. I rarely select a color solely for its fun or trendiness. There's a way to intentionally choose and distribute colors throughout a space to ensure that they don't quickly grow tiresome or feel overwhelming. If you are a novice with color or have been intimidated by it, start small. Get to know the different colors that speak to you and how they play with other colors. After years of studying and a lifetime of living with this design element, I tend to look at color in a specific way. I consider color as a palette, not as a singular hue. Let's look at pale pink, for instance. I think about how it will work with another pink for a monochromatic palette *and* how it will work with a contrasting tone like dark green or even caramel. A palette doesn't necessarily include only two colors. Regardless of saturation (how strong or weak the color is), two colors should welcome a third. A tertiary color mellows a room so it can breathe. Also, when you think about a palette, think about what you want to serve as the neutral. The foil of a neutral is what keeps colors palatable.

WHERE TO FIND COLOR

Outdoors

When I use the word *outdoors*, you may be jumping to thoughts of natural elements such as a body of water or the countryside. That's one way to

There are color palettes everywhere. Their familiarity in food makes certain dishes jumping-off points for ideas.

think about the outdoors, and by all means, I encourage you to lose yourself among rolling hills and the open road by riding a train or cruising in the car. There's much to be learned from a drive.

What if you're in a metropolis like New York City? A short stroll outside over a handful of city blocks can stimulate you with the yellow of taxicabs, the gunmetal gray of the buildings, and colors of neon if you're basking in the lights and action of Times Square. Sure, urban settings are chock-full of visuals; it's not all about mass population. I'm also thinking about what it might be like to walk around the square in Santa Fe, New Mexico. The sand and terra-cotta hues of adobe buildings in the Southwest just might be the optimal combination for a family room in need of warmth. Then there's Charleston, South Carolina. Stroll down Rainbow Row with a refreshing sweet

tea in hand and you'll be charmed by glorious pastels that bathe the iconic street of historic houses.

Food

Pay a visit to the local greenmarket wherever you may be. Today's produce aisles display a wide spectrum of colorful foods. Just when you thought that carrots were orange, you will see them in yellow and purple, too. Cauliflower now matches the fresh foliage of spring in a new chartreuse variety.

Restaurants are also a good source of color palettes. After all, a piece of chicken on its own may not be all that exciting. But rest it on a puree of golden butternut squash or drizzle it with a luscious green pesto, and all of a sudden, a piece of brown chicken can look as delicious as it tastes. Wondering whether an all-white room can be accented with both red and green? It certainly works on a lobster roll, where succulent lobster is finished with snippets of chive.

The point is, there are color palettes everywhere. Their familiarity in food makes certain dishes jumping-off points for ideas. You may not mix all of the colors together in the same proportions at home, and maybe you'll use the colors in different values (shades or tint of the colors), but you will know that they can work together.

Shopping

I always want to bring a memento home from a trip, so I carve out time to shop at design stores, clothing boutiques, antiques shops, and markets. Their color palettes can be reflective of the region, so shopping can stamp an exclamation point on a destination's look. When I'm in Morocco, I stuff my suitcase with colorful caftans, baskets, and babouches from the souk.

Maybe it is a new garment, or maybe a flea market find that inspires you. Whether you bring a memento home with you or merely snap a picture of it on your phone, color entices on your shopping trips and inspires you later on.

Keep in mind that travel doesn't necessarily require a plane ticket to some faraway land. A Sunday drive to the country twenty minutes from your home or an afternoon trip downtown in your city can deliver a new appreciation for the local hues in your surroundings.

The Things That You Use

It's my observation that people who are enthusiastic about design carry that enthusiasm to all forms of it, whether public and imposing things or more personal and smaller-scale objects. I have always been a collector of stationery and I love desk supplies. Practical items such as folders, boxes, notepads, labels, and planners help keep my projects colorfully organized and efficient. I could buy basic versions of necessities and they would serve the same function. Or would they? Since I prefer versions of office supplies in visually interesting forms and colors, I find joy every time I use them. There are so many pretty color schemes on folders, boxes, and every other office supply.

Another place where I find color inspiration is in packaging. I especially enjoy looking at tea tins and boxes, cosmetics, perfumes, and even wine bottles. Next time you're wandering the grocery or department store, take a minute not to buy, but to examine the packaging. Bath and cleaning products and candles are also good sources of well-designed packaging. Remember, we can find inspiration everywhere.

CREATING A MOOD BOARD

Developing a palette takes a bit of research, and trial and error. However, let's be honest, it's the most fun kind. I like to build a mood board when creating a design scheme. My guess is that once you start to start tearing, pinning, and filing color inspirations you will enjoy the process. I'll also bet that you've already started a mood board, even if you don't realize it. Take a look at your social media. Do you have accounts on Pinterest

ABOVE *Slight alterations of traditional palettes are what keep design interesting. Here, a tartan shoe demonstrates that blue is as deserving of a spot in the Christmas palette as red and green.*

OPPOSITE *Imagination is the key to turning the function of a piece into something new. A wool plaid throw doubles as a tablecloth for a fall gathering.*

and Instagram? Swipe through the pictures on your phone. I know that a significant number of images are saved to your phone merely because you find beauty in them. Think about adding those to a mood board.

Remember, mood boards are not solely about paint chips, fabric swatches, and finish samples. If you are inspired by a piece of wrapping paper or a pretty ribbon, add it. Secure a piece of jewelry to the board as you think about design. You can always store it back with your other jewelry later. Maybe a dream car or vacation is what inspires you. Add pictures of those, too.

A mood board should be joyful.

As you start building your mood board, keep looking at how it collectively forms. You will naturally start to edit, identifying favorite bits on the board and noting that others can be removed. A mood board should be joyful. Don't think of it as an intimidating assignment. There's no right or wrong answer when it comes to what you love.

COLOR IN CONTEXT

There many colors and values to choose from, so I want to deep dive into my thoughts on specific hues. I won't be able to address every color here, but these are a few that I think require some guidance.

Pink

It's the color of sunsets, peonies, roses, and watermelon and has been threaded throughout the ages. In the United States, navy blue is a go-to that is neutral and represents stability. Pink has always been known as "the navy blue of India" and can easily be a neutral when it's juxtaposed with other hues. Pink-and-white is crisp and clean. Every shade of pink with every shade of green is a win for me, emphasized perhaps with a

touch of yellow. It's the color combination that I chose for my business logo. For a sporty scheme, pair pink with red or orange. For a preppy look, combine pink with navy. Pink doesn't have to be girly. Sure, when we think about pink, a little girl's spring dress may come to mind. But think of a soft, muddy pink on a dapper men's shirt or tie. Pink can be a bold head-turner and it can be elegant and sophisticated.

A main event pattern like the tree-of-life motif on these drapery panels informs colors for furniture and painted pieces.

When a house has an open format, it's important to make sure that adjoining rooms speak to each other with a cohesive palette.

LEFT *Neutral palettes tend to be loaded with texture. Here, grass cloth–covered walls, a raffia lampshade, and a rattan chair complement the lively patterns of the rug and stools.*

OPPOSITE *When feelings of warmth and comfort are a priority, a mix of neutral tones will make the room glow.*

Natural Colors

Before you conjure specific colors in your head, consider this: When the word *natural* is used to describe color, it doesn't tell the entire story. We tend to think of subdued dirty colors and browns, sage green, and grays when we think of a "natural palette." I encourage everyone to use the word *earthy* for those colors instead. Natural colors encompass those that you might not have considered. Your trip to a farmers market or a sit on a garden bench will prove that. We tend to automatically dismiss saturated colors with strong intensities as unnatural, but in fact, they are the color of strawberries, carrots, blueberries, and pineapple. In the garden, marigolds, gerbera daisies, and blue hydrangeas are bright among others. Use the word *natural* cautiously when referencing color to professionals, because they will need additional information. There's a difference between the colors of nature and soft, earthy colors.

Black and Brown

Both these colors are essential, but they can deliver different moods. Black can be edgy, clean, and graphic. Brown is soft and warm. While you might not see a lot of black in my rooms, this color can be vital in terms of grounding a space and playing off other bright colors in a room. For instance, if you are going to place a pair of velvet sofas in a jewel tone like teal, consider a brown coffee table to ground them. If I added another saturated color to that scheme, I would confuse the eye. Brown anchors and provides relief.

Not everything needs to be colorful. In fact, eliminating color in spots—as we've done here by pairing the bright sofas with a neutral rug and wood coffee table—lets the eye rest.

Working with White

A handsome color scheme of stone should be defined by another color. Here, black does the trick, emphasizing the perimeter of the powder room and accessories.

I prefer walls that are a color versus ones that are white. Other people feel the opposite, and that's fine, too. To me, it's all about the colors and contrast or lack thereof. If we are designing a room that is both sculptural and textural, with bouclé textiles and high-gloss paint on the ceiling, then white can live on the walls. You can create an entire room that way. Texture helps balance the color.

People tend to think that when we imagine a clean, uninhabited space, that means antiseptic white. White symbolizes something fresh, pure, and clean. It signifies serenity. However, white can be used intentionally as a color. If there's a lot of texture, that is what's noticed, more than the color itself.

All-white spaces have flooded social media in recent years, and, yes, they can be serenely beautiful. Ask yourself this, though: Are you attracted to a space because it is all white or because it is monotone? Remember, you can create a monotone look in any color, not just white.

In the end, white can be stunning. If you choose an all-white look, use materials that reflect the light differently. Alabaster, for instance, can be elegant, warm, and beautifully enhance the sculptural aspect of a lamp.

ABOVE *When they are splashed with color, ceilings can make a room more intimate, as in this entry foyer.*

LEFT *Arresting architecture should be matched with design elements of equal magnitude. A rug of oversized concentric squares not only balances the vaulted ceiling, but also directs the room's color scheme.*

PUTTING PALETTE INTO PRACTICE

Creativity in the imagination should be endless and without limits. At some point, though, it's important to identify steps and a process to bring your ideas to fruition. Not every designer uses the same process, but I want to share the one that has worked for me.

The tried and true, old-school way to launch a palette is with a colorful rug. Oftentimes, threads of many colors are incorporated into a rug, so there are several options to pull from. I take a somewhat different approach.

Step One. Establish a palette that feels good. Here's a little tip that I learned early in my career: Think about how your home would appear if all the walls fell down. Your home should have a palette that is harmonious and relevant overall. It doesn't necessarily have to showcase the same colors in every space, but it needs similar color values and weights to form a cohesive look, one with continuity and symmetry.

Step Two. Once I decide if a color scheme is going to be saturated or subdued, I choose a main-event element. It could be a Persian rug, a wallpaper, even a dynamic piece of artwork. The main event is important because it's what will drive accessories, such as a small piece of furniture or a pair of lamps.

Step Three. Add accent colors. Accents play an important role in palettes because they can easily send a palette in a different direction. The obvious place for them is on throw pillows, where you can use a special fabric in small doses. Also turn to lamps, vases, drapery trims, or linens in the bedroom to introduce another color into the mix. In a kitchen, an island in a contrasting color can accent the room. If your cabinets have glass fronts, pay attention to glassware and consider colored versions that draw attention with style.

ABOVE *Thinking outside the box for a table setting usually results in a positive first impression and spirited conversation. Here, a Fourth of July–themed table pivots from loads of obvious stars and stripes to one star plate that tops a bevy of appropriate but unexpected motifs.*

OPPOSITE *What makes a scheme interesting is presenting something in a unique manner. Red, white, and blue, usually used in the middle of summer, is rendered here with florals and spongeware. If you aren't hosting a Fourth of July celebration, forgo the stars and stripes for patterns that you love.*

BEYOND SEASONAL SCHEMES

When thinking about personal and signature colors, I like to think outside of what's expected. It's normal for colors to be defined seasonally, but they don't have to be. In today's world, we feel free to wear all colors all year round and live with them, too. Materials matter, so white linen is very different than a white brushed wool. In a coastal room, blue might be ideal in a crisp cotton stripe. A velvet version applied to a chair allows the color to exist effortlessly in a floor-to-ceiling wood-paneled library with a fire crackling.

Winter white is a great example of an unexpected seasonal color. A cozy white fisherman's sweater on a blizzardy day tempers the darkness of the year's coldest time. In the fall, a velvet lavender-and-green printed jacket can morph into an autumnal palette, although the color scheme might be more expected at another time of year.

Again, I reference fashion because it shows color on a smaller scale than furnishings and can adapt rather quickly. Remember to train your eye to see colors and patterns as a whole, not individually. Consider all surroundings and avoid designing in a bubble. Take color away from its calendar month for a scheme that is custom to you.

How color makes us feel might seem like a cliché, but it's very real. The delightful moments of life and the way that we are inspired, encouraged, and calmed are extremely important. Color affects us, whether we consciously acknowledge it or not. We should choose color for its mood; its moment in time; for its style; and ultimately, for its joy.

LEFT *Chances are your closet is loaded with inspiration for your interiors. Don't review only your garments. Take a peek at your accessories, too, like the striped belt here, to inform your selections.*

OPPOSITE *Contrast is a primary tool when it comes to making color statements. I make it a priority to find a color for the architectural trim and moldings to offset whatever hue covers the walls or siding.*

chapter 3

CREATING
WOW MOMENTS:
PUSHING
THE ENVELOPE

ABOVE AND OPPOSITE *A simple detail like trim painted in a color other than white offers an opportunity to define a room's attitude.*

PAGE 72 *Color can be an easy way to create a wow moment and is a go-to when a space calls for pizzazz. A mood board is a helpful tool to make sure that a scheme doesn't become too bold or overwhelming.*

A main event is part of a complete design's formula. It's what I build from and oftentimes what inspires the appointments of my interiors. A *wow moment*, on the other hand, isn't part of any formula—in fact, it's the time when things go offtrack. A wow moment is a surprise and gives license to break the rules and what's expected.

It's likely your home has been the setting for plenty of wow moments, yet maybe not all in the design sense. Whether they are holidays, large milestones, or small triumphs, our lives are all about the moments that bring a joyful spirit to every day.

Your home, in turn, deserves high notes here and there, too. Wow moments are opportunities to rethink spaces that need a pick-me-up. As you'll see in this chapter, you can get creative with what you have or reinvent things altogether. When the mood strikes, just remember: With a little imagination, you can update a room just about any time.

HOW TO WOW

Inspiration is everywhere, and chances are you have found it while traveling, shopping, or even when dining in a chic restaurant. Maybe it's the designer in me or just my innate wanderlust, but I'm constantly taking inspiration from my surroundings. Often, it's an idea that never would have emerged without that particular glimpse of the world: seeing sea turtles swimming in the blue waters of the Bahamas, visiting museums in Venice, coming around the corner of a narrow street in Florence and seeing the Duomo against the sky. Experiences such as these stay in our mind's eye.

ABOVE *Successful design isn't about being shy. When I apply lattice to a wall, I approach it with a maximalist attitude, adding another layer with bold artwork.*

LEFT *Impact comes from layering. Here, bright white lattice contrasts the solid color wall underneath. Caned chairs and a crystal chandelier add texture among the bold hues.*

When I'm trying to use my inspiration—whatever it may be—to design a wow moment, I always ask myself a few questions to provide a little framework. Ask yourself these same questions and watch your impressive creativity unfold.

• **Is it unique?** When I'm finalizing interiors on a project, and the rugs are unrolled, the furniture is situated, and the artwork and accessories are placed, I delight in the big reveal. I cherish those unveilings. The icing on the cake, of course, is the moment when the homeowners notice a vignette and say, "I love what you did here. I never would have thought of that." You don't have to reinvent the wheel to find a wow moment—take inspiration from something that you've seen or experienced and use your own lens to create a detail that you love.

• **Does it hold its own?** In a room design, a wow moment is a little surprise that is self-contained and not reliant on the other parts of the room: It is strong enough to stand on its own.

For example, I highlighted a doorway with peacock blue paint to create a double frame effect for the painting that was visible as you entered the home. No other details are needed to complete the vignette. No big room, collection of knickknacks, or overbearing details are required. The vignette, balanced and curated, stood on its own. A wow moment never needs a sidekick.

• **Is it unexpected?** Some parts of every design are tried and true—whether color palette, furniture arrangement, or displayed collection—and they should be. Reserve the surprise for one spot, and then make it happen by giving something conventional a twist to make it *unconventional*.

Here's an example. Substitute framed textiles for a painting or sketch to hang above a console table. There are so many gorgeous choices—and when you tap into antique textiles, they become even more interesting. How lovely to be reminded of a trip by displaying a pretty fabric souvenir. Another unexpected artwork installation: Enlarge and frame a photograph of a favorite item to give it presence.

ABOVE *A skirted table is a hallmark of traditional style. This console has an updated version, made of wicker to keep the waves of the skirt stable. A silk scarf on the wall above adds a luxurious touch.*

OPPOSITE *When it comes to florals, a loose pattern like the one I chose for this sofa and window treatment gives the room movement with its airy and open depiction.*

LEFT *When black and white is the centerpiece of a room's scheme, not much else is needed. I like to use stripes in attic spaces and in other nooks with architectural angles.*

OPPOSITE *When scheming a room in black and white, consider softening the graphic appearance with a pattern like this feathery fern frond wallpaper.*

With so many nooks and crannies, I had to choose what was destined to be the zinger in this loft office. The striped floor treatment creates impact and is a simple DIY project that can easily be accomplished over a weekend.

CREATING DOMINANT POINTS

Designers understand the need for dominant points throughout a house. Figuring out where they should be proves to be a more of a challenge. Here are a few suggestions that work for me.

• **Highlight the architecture.** Look for niches, structural framing, a floating wall, built-ins, or a lowered ceiling or elevated room to make your mark. Mantels also lend themselves to a noteworthy vignette. If there is no focal point in a room, create one by adding a chest of drawers or console table with a pair of lamps and artwork.

• **Take a walk.** That's right. Stroll through your house and watch for points, especially in large rooms, that beg for stylish interruptions.

• **Start small.** Since the powder room is typically a small space and is also a room visited frequently by guests, why not make it a jewel box standout? Add surprise with an array of patterns, textures, and even colors. Try using a material on the countertop that you wouldn't dream of using in a large space, or find a glamorous lighting fixture with an abundance of sparkle. Make the powder room the star.

DESIGN PRINCIPLES

Contrast

Imagine a classic blue-and-white room with traditional furniture upholstered in mattress ticking stripe. There are several ways to think about next steps. There is the English, highly matched route where everything (you guessed it) is in the same fabric and the painting above the fireplace blends in with the surroundings. Or there's the more surprising route, in which you add a jolt of color with an abstract painting that's an unapologetic pivot from the scheme. This is *contrast*.

Contrast is an ideal tool to achieve the wow moment, because in a way it provides you with the answer. In general, it's safe to choose the opposite of what's already going on in the room. A room with black walls, for instance, is striking with crisp white trim. A sun-room drenched in

Soft palettes can be dynamic, too. The oversized tree-of-life pattern in this powder room commands attention.

An unexpected color pairing will open minds and eyes. Here, a cheerful cherry red pops against aqua for a sophisticated take on red and blue.

A vestibule relies on shocking pink to pique curiosity and lure us in to enjoy a zebra painting. I always consider using a bold color behind artwork that floats without a frame.

ABOVE *Black and warm ivory naturally lend a graphic note to a vignette. Sometimes I'll use the combo to grab attention and then show a dynamic piece of artwork like this painting. The console table is encased in natural material; the bench shows off a pattern with tribal influences.*

OPPOSITE *Spark a classic combination like blue and white with something strong and unexpected. Here an abstract in contrasting colors creates drama.*

fresh greens to extend the gardens indoors can be dramatic and empowering when interrupted with a pair of bright pink lamps or an armoire in lemon yellow. A living room in a center hall colonial house with strong millwork and Regency furniture only gets better when thrown the curve ball of a modern cocktail table or streamlined lighting.

Contrast in design is the opportunity to really see each piece for the personality that it has, and that means occasionally taking an unexpected path to a new color family, a new historical era, or a new genre. Contrast in design empowers us by showing that it's not only OK to be different but what's *preferred* to make a space zestful.

Treatment

Treatment is the way you treat a surface or bring it to the forefront. And it's a tool that I find useful when I want to take something ordinary and necessary and turn it into some special.

Favorite spots of mine that can add a bit of zest to a room are floors and ceilings. These two surfaces offer blank canvases to dazzle, so I always keep them in mind from the get-go for interesting treatment.

Is the floor made of wood that's not in tiptop shape? Set aside the natural solution—to refinish with a new stain. Instead, paint your flooring. For instance, I once chose a trio of colors to stripe the existing floor of a loft space that served as a home office for an artist. The floor palette was graphic and showed creativity, but in an orderly manner.

Treatment is a design concept that I think about when I start with a basic: simple linen drapery panels in need of a border or trim, or a pillow that begs for a flange. Think about ways to elevate design elements.

Styling for Impact

Styling is something I do instinctively. It is the process of adding accessories and is necessary everywhere throughout a home, although the goal is to make the space look natural and not overdone. I always remember the following:

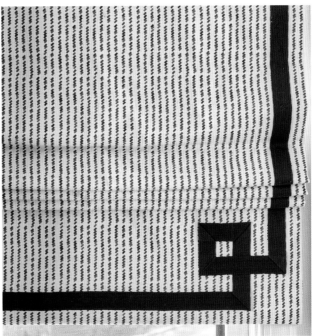

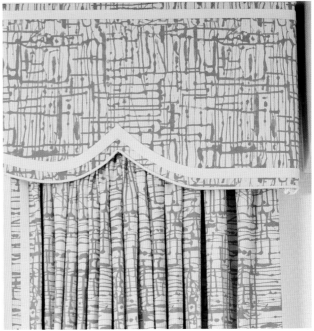

ABOVE *Basic drapery panels can remain simple but stylish when edged with a contrasting trim.*

OPPOSITE *Architecture has presence even in its most simple form: The painted window trim highlights the room's bold palette.*

TOP *Details at the window make sure that, whether the shades are open or shut, there is something pretty to see. Navy tape makes a solid contrast to the broken red stripes.*

BOTTOM *A valance-and-panel treatment can be a chic enhancement to a beautiful view outdoors.*

When you want to create a wow moment, think big. Styling a wow moment relies on scale, mass, and nature.

Using scale

Art is a passion of mine. I'm attracted to pieces of all kinds, but when I acquire a large piece of my own or am given the opportunity to work with one for a client it's a game changer.

Something large-scale, whether it's artwork, a grand étagère, or a sexy long curved sofa, causes one to pause and notice. Consider oversized lamps to add a sculptural touch to a hallway, or a large bowl filled with artichokes to add volume to a kitchen island. Even better, give the bowl the friend of a tall vase and corral both on an oversized tray so the mix reads as one cohesive unit.

Using mass

There is power in numbers. Sometimes an object is not special on its own, but in multiples it creates sculpture. I always think about numbers when I'm buying ceramics, pottery, ginger jars, vases, and bowls. Here's a tip: If everything is similar in color, go ahead and vary the shapes and sizes. For instance, I love a garniture of jars or tea canisters in different heights.

ABOVE RIGHT *Overhead lighting has become dual purpose. Not only does it provide a light, it also acts as a decorative sculpture.*

RIGHT *Statement pieces are best placed in spots where they can stand alone and draw attention.*

OPPOSITE *Soaring architecture can be enough to turn heads but can also accommodate daring ensembles of furniture forms, colors, and an assortment of patterns.*

A bookcase or shelving unit is an ideal piece to introduce height. Here, one with a fretwork frame adds a moment of garden flair.

Beyond the Paint: Lattice or Treillage

Lattice, which creates texture and depth on its own, is pushed forward by color that's painted on the wall behind it. A third contrasting accent, fuchsia, draws the eye further.

It's no secret that I have an affinity for Palm Beach and its impeccably cheerful design hallmarks. One in particular that I can't get enough of is lattice on the walls, ceiling, or on both. With sunshine beaming down on most days, the mainstay neutral of Palm Beach is white. It looks fresh when paired with myriad bright colors that Palm Beach embraces and encourages. But why rely on paint alone when it can be boosted with the application of treillage? Lattice delivers so many of the concepts that I talk about throughout this book: depth, layering, contrast, texture, and more. For this treatment, even as a colorist, I'm perfectly willing to layer white trellis over a plain white wall. But when I aim to take the design up yet another notch, I splash a bright color of paint over the walls first, which can peek through the lattice after it's applied.

Lattice is an ideal upgrade for a garden room or sun-room. I'm always searching for a place to extend the beauty of the outdoors. And rain or shine, summer or winter, lattice references the great outdoors that we long to live with. Think about other rooms, too. How lovely would it be to begin each morning with a cup of coffee while sitting on a banquette where lattice has been applied to the surrounding walls? Or to end the day in a latticed dining room? Applying lattice is a sure way to add depth and a terrific conversation starter, too.

A bold abstract painting grabs attention but doesn't completely steal the show. It's accompanied by an array of colors and patterns to emphasize its dominance.

Another go-to of mine is colored woodwork and built-ins. I'm imagining a wonderful sage-colored or dark green unit that houses a collection of English creamware. The contrast would be powerful and would tell the story of something special that is collected and personal.

Using nature

Who doesn't love flowers? They bring instant beauty to a space, along with life and softness. The best source for dynamic moments is Mother Nature. I can't think of a more delightful way to create a wow moment than with flowers.

CREATIVITY

In design, creativity may seem obvious, but it's not always. There's no definite stopping point for creativity, but the following two categories are good places to start.

Make Artwork a Priority

Wow-moment artwork doesn't have to be expensive. It doesn't have to be auction-worthy or even an investment. It just has to be a piece that you love. Here's how to make it a star.

• **Fashion a gallery wall.** This is an ideal treatment to optimize a collection of disparate works. Select frames in a similar color family and tone for all the pieces. Some people like the graphic presence of works of a similar size. Other people like the interest when the pieces vary in size. Either way, the more framed pieces, the bigger the impact.

• **Let a single piece be.** If you have a work of art that is sizable or important, consider letting it live on its own, no matter how big or small. When there is something of prominence, it doesn't necessarily need the noise of additional objects. Its minimalistic display will have visitors asking why.

• **Keep friends together.** When there is a group of artwork that feels best in unison, display it that way. Repetition is much like symmetry. It's soothing to the eye. A grouping of multiple coordinating pieces shows commitment and confidence.

ABOVE *Amassing a collection of like objects is one way to make a statement. A set of dishes in the same pattern gives presence to a tablescape.*

OPPOSITE *A symmetrical and quiet moment can become something special with a stately flower arrangement. I love orchids for their color variety and low-maintenance care.*

Geometrics add instant pop. I use them when I want to imbue a room with energy. Here, I took a cue from the chevron floor pattern and found artwork to keep the electric spirit going.

TOP LEFT *Use nature as inspiration for artwork: These painted leaves steal the show. Or, instead of paintings, why not collect autumn leaves—or fallen leaves from a special trip—then frame and display them?*

LEFT *A grouping of artwork can create the same scale and volume on a wall as a single large piece. Framing everything in the same manner makes the display cohesive.*

ABOVE *Artwork doesn't have to be displayed against white or black walls. Here, coral pink creates a fashionable backdrop for coordinating pieces.*

OPPOSITE *A pretty grouping of small works of art can be more powerful than one piece on its own. I routinely place them over a patterned wallpaper that enhances the colors and gives the art additional importance.*

OPPOSITE *The sharp value of chartreuse puts a fashionable spin on more polite hues such as soft pink. The statement pattern used on the upholstered pieces here is heightened with draperies that highlight its bright yellow accents.*

ABOVE *Lighting offers an ideal spot to think about a statement finish, especially on a classic shape. This one bears an abstract glaze that is offset by a cheerful patterned shade.*

Placement

You might not consider wallpaper, even if it's a bold statement pattern, to be unusual. But what if it was used as a layer in an unusual place other than a wall?

Get your feet wet with a design that's a little daring in a small space first. Little nooks and other spaces, like walk-in closets, prove the ideal laboratory in which to try something new without the commitment that's required in a space with larger proportions.

For the walk-in closet of a primary bedroom, I always want the space to be as fashionable as the garments that it houses. A favorite walk-in closet of mine is one where I applied a blue cherry-branch-printed grass cloth on the ceiling, which ties in with the blue of the center island.

Reaching the wow moment requires letting go of what you think should be. It's about breaking the rules and breaking the norm just enough to draw attention. Sometimes it makes sense, but it really does not have to. Remember, when you hear those magic words, "I wouldn't have thought of that," that's when you know that your design is impactful. Moments of wow are the lessons that prove all that is possible.

RIGHT *Look up! Chances are that you might see something special, like the cherry blossom statement pattern stretched over the ceiling, which I used as inspiration for the center island.*

OPPOSITE *Small spaces, like this walk-in closet, are the perfect spot to try a design that is a little daring.*

chapter 4

LAYERING AND THE DETAILS THAT MAKE AN IMPRESSION

ABOVE AND OPPOSITE *It's so easy to bring home small, portable souvenirs from traveling or shopping expeditions. Keep scale in mind for such displays, to visually offset little trinkets.*

PAGE 106 *Green and brown is such a natural color scheme, but it doesn't have to feel earthy. Olive and hunter green reminds us of libraries and imbues a serious tone. To lighten the mood, add a dab of light blue.*

We are all familiar with the concept of teamwork and the idea that the sum of our collective ideas is greater than any specific one. Interior design follows the same concept, and it comes in the form of layering.

Layering is a symphonic blend of elements and a time-lapse picture of our visual creativity. It evolves and builds a decorative scheme that makes our home interesting. When we layer, our home turns into a memory box that documents a life lived through the acquisitions and collections that we find dear.

My hope is that this chapter gives you confidence to routinely look at your home, critique it, and consider what's next. Layering is fun. It encourages trial and error and allows for us to make mistakes that can be somewhat easily corrected. Weaving details both big and small into a space gives us permission to decorate in stages. You never have to be finished and can continue to dream, play, and add—then repeat those steps all over again.

Layering isn't about design rules. Instead, it's about what feels good to the eye. Most important, layering is the design tool that will make your home personal.

Florals and geometrics are a tried-and-true pairing. Here, a bold floral adds a moment of garden beauty against geometric wallpaper and a coordinating armchair.

*Layering works when pieces around a room
reference each other. The lemon-yellow lamp on
the buffet pulls color from the decorative trim
on the drapery panels.*

A unified palette enhances the view from one room into another: Striped chairs in the living room are emphasized by green window panels in the adjacent room.

THE LAYERING PROCESS

Layering Versus Styling

Let's start with some design vocabulary. It's important that as you think about your own design schemes, you have a clear understanding of these terms.

Layering can sometimes be mistakenly confused with styling. In the hierarchy of design, layering ranks far closer to the top. For both my personal and professional projects, layering begins on day one and can include building materials before the decorative work ever starts.

I'll deep dive into specific components throughout this chapter, but architectural elements, lighting, and the architecture itself must address layering from the very get-go. Layering the architecture affects the flow of a house and the way that a house functions. Decorative layering affects the personality of the interiors, keeping them from becoming too expected and looking like a showroom or retail space.

Styling is a part of the layering process that occurs near the end and addresses how the smaller roving elements land throughout your rooms. The styling part of layering can withstand regular adjustment with ease. It's likely that you've assigned larger pieces of furniture to specific spots in each room. Smaller furniture, however, such as ceramic stools, drink tables, tray tables, and an extra small chair, are mobile and can be major players in styling.

Determining Room Objectives
Rooms for lots of people

Since layering starts at the very beginning, it's important for you to think about what you want your room to accomplish. It's most important that a room not only exude beauty but make the people who are in it feel comfortable. Think about rooms that need to accommodate a lot of people, because where there are people, there needs to be seating and surfaces to serve them.

A large living room or family room is simple to deal with when it comes to providing ample

opportunities to sit. It's likely that there is a sofa or sectional that anchors your space, along with several chairs. If you have a room of smaller proportions, you might consider the following options. Instead of a hard-surface cocktail table, invest in an upholstered piece. It can make shift as seating, too, and when you need a stable surface to keep a drink from tipping over, you can top it with a chic tray. A pair of stools can find a home under a console table when they are not in use. If this is something that you might be interested in, think about buying stools on casters for a smoother slide.

In both instances, not only are you tackling the seating challenge head on, but by adding extra stools, tables, and ottomans, you are inadvertently layering. A console table with nothing underneath it leaves empty space. There's nothing wrong with that, but it's also an opportunity to build visual interest so the vignette is not solely about the console table, rather the collective statement of a variety of pieces. The same is true of an ottoman. While I personally enjoy styling the solid surface of a cocktail table too, it doesn't need a tray on top of it. An upholstered ottoman does, and that's an opportunity to add a few books and maybe a favorite object. This is layering.

ABOVE *Much like picture frames that show off your favorite people, a cocktail table's surface is front and center to display your favorite things.*

OPPOSITE *Bright and cheerful spaces in light colors, like the creamy ivory and blue here, need a moment of visual shift. A brown side table adds weight beside the sofa.*

Rooms that need to look good at night

Certain rooms are used at various times of the day, but ones that are used at night need to address layering differently.

The dining room, for instance, is usually not a high-traffic area within a home, yet it emits drama, glamour, and illumination like no other space. It's where we tend to look our best, dressed up for a family holiday or a stylish event with friends. Dining rooms aren't always used at night, but usually a dinner party occurs as the sun goes down or afterward. There are a lot of layering requirements that accompany a dining room due the plethora of special things used to style a tablescape. Cloths, placemats, dinnerware, flatware, centerpiece elements, and an array of glasses that sparkle in the light of a chandelier deliver visual excitement.

Then there's the lighting. In rooms that are used mostly at night, layering the lighting scheme creates a certain mood and affects how everyone looks. In the dining room, a primary fixture like a chandelier is important for its drama, but so are wall sconces, as they will distribute light around the room while guests are seated during the meal or standing for cocktails before. On a buffet piece, think about adding a pair of ceramic lamps on either side to cast a pretty glow on what is placed there.

Rooms that are hardworking

I approach layering differently for kitchens and bathrooms. Lighting in such spaces requires careful consideration to make sure that you can see what you are doing in there. Task lighting is likely something that you want to be low-profile and inconspicuous, with decorative pieces commanding more attention.

Another consideration is the number of things that you use to layer. For instance, living rooms are full of decorative objects, travel finds, and books. You probably use a living room or family room to sit in, relax, and maybe read. Think about what you can handle, though, in a more functional space. In your home office for example, too many objects may interfere with your ability to focus. In a kitchen, I like to add useful pieces that are attractive, too. Cutting or serving boards aged to beauty, large ceramic or wood bowls that can corral fresh fruit, and trays are ideal pieces to layer with. Remember, in a kitchen there is grease, oil, and lots of splashes that you might not always catch. So too many things can be a hassle to clean in the long run.

Incorporating Visual and Tactile Moments

Layering requires confidence to keep going. I find that sometimes people who I'm working with can be a tad shy when it comes to the building-layers part of the design process. I oftentimes hear, "I struggle with knowing if things go together." I understand, and think that layering can be a challenge for those who only understand a design

Styling is a part of the layering process that occurs near the end and addresses how the smaller roving elements land throughout your rooms.

where everything matches. If you find building different moments difficult, I encourage you to keep going. Your eyes will let you know when it's time to stop.

Much of layering has to do with the mix of visual and tactile elements. You will naturally have hard surfaces in your rooms that, if nothing else, come from the walls, ceiling, and floor. When there are hard surfaces, you'll want to introduce elements to soften the scheme. Upholstery fabrics help that, but you might still need a throw blanket or throw pillows. That's easy in a family room, not so much in a kitchen. That's why the addition of something with warm tones, like cutting boards or the mottled glaze of a big bowl, can temper the hard lines there. Similarly,

OPPOSITE *The dark tones of a cocktail table complement other rich tones such as handsome blacks, grays, and deep red.*

In a classic, traditional room, layering a natural material like these matchstick shades brings a casual and carefree vibe to the space.

in a bathroom, textured things such as towels, robes hung on hooks, and soaps or bath salts in shapely jars can balance the visual prominence of the vanity top, cabinets, and plumbing fixtures.

Building the Goods to Layer With

Once decorative choices for the hard building elements of the rooms such as the walls and wallpaper, flooring, and hardwired lighting are in place, it's time to start building the movable parts. As for what to buy, here are a couple of guidelines that I find helpful:

• **Consider scale.** One mistake that I often see people make is using too many small objects. They can be difficult to see, causing visual confusion. Large-scale accessories are necessary to bridge the space between the big furniture and anything small in a room. Layering requires small steps between sizes of elements. A big basket for throws or games, a large bowl on a cocktail table, and oversized books are good places to start. Layering creates a gradual hierarchy among elements to keep the look from having too much contrast or being jarring.

• **Buy in bulk.** Build your collection by buying multiples. I've been there myself at a design shop or antiquing. I see something that I would love to have in my home and debate whether I should buy just one or multiples to make a statement. If there are different sizes of a piece such as a vase or, in the case of vintage and antique pieces, significant inventory of the same look, consider buying more than one. I find it helpful to take a moment in a shop or booth to think about how interesting a piece is on its own, and what it might look like as part of a collection. You can also go one step farther and determine where the collection might live in your home.

Here's an example: I personally love creamware, and some of the homeowners who I help do, too. I'm prone to finishing cabinetry in a saturated color, and a collection of creamware

looks bright and cheerful against a contrasting hue. Keep in mind that this layering treatment builds a graphic contrast that can make antique finds more modern. Of course, you can achieve a similar look with new things, too.

SCHEMING A ROOM WITH FABRICS AND PATTERNS

If you share my enthusiasm for design, you are drawn to so many components: arresting architecture, striking forms, and artwork that mesmerizes with beauty. There are two categories, however, that captivate me more than the others, to where I get lost in the experience of reviewing them, and they are fabrics and wallpapers.

In the TV world, people binge-watch in their leisure time. I, similarly, travel down the rabbit hole of bins and books that are brimming with fabric and wallpaper samples. There's no part of the design process that I find more captivating

One mistake that I often see people make is using too many small objects. They can be difficult to see, causing visual confusion.

and charming. There's color and pattern and, most important, style. With so many fabrics and wallpapers to choose from, it's easy to get lost in the possibilities and allow the inventory to keep you from making decisions. I have a couple of tips, though, to keep the process moving.

The Main Event

There are so many words to describe the pattern that directs everything else—*dominant, primary, leading.* All are accurate descriptors. On my team, we use the term "main event" as part of our design lexicon. To be clear, a main event doesn't have to be a textile or wallcovering. A rug, piece of art, even a memorable piece of marble can be a main event. In my design, though, patterned textiles and

OPPOSITE *Dining room built-ins with varying heights and surfaces allow for interesting styling around the food that will be served. Add something live, such as plants or branches, that will enhance but not compete with centerpiece flowers.*

LEFT *Graphic displays are not reserved for modern schemes. Paint a traditional cabinet, then fill it with objects that create a strong contrast. This cabinet frames a collection of English creamware.*

OPPOSITE *Layering doesn't have to be loud. Against a cross-hatch wall, soft additions such as a neutral geometric chair, a chinoiserie ginger jar, and light-blue trim on the shades create interest but aren't glaring.*

wallcoverings are somewhat of a hallmark of my look. Plus, I enjoy the process of layering lots of patterns, so it's likely that when I'm starting from scratch, I will look for a main event in these two categories.

Main event patterns have a strong point of view. By *strong* I mean that they have a distinct attitude when it comes to color, scale, or the pattern itself. A grand floral with curvy vines sprinkled with birds and butterflies could be a main event pattern. The same is true of a graphic chevron in fashion-forward tones such as shocking pink and black. The main event fabric plays the leading role in a space, with coordinating prints, colors, and objects to support it. Also keep in mind that a solid can be a main event, too. Think about a room that's painted white, with straight apple green panels at the windows. This look is edited and modern, but still striking.

As you go searching for a statement fabric, here's my advice. If you are attracted to patterns, look at them the same way that you do pieces of art. That's what patterns are, after all. Flip through fabric books or large lengths of fabric if you have access to a showroom. Once you settle on your main event, the rest will help build a look that is custom to you.

The Coordinates

After you've settled on a main event pattern, it's time to search for supporting characters. This can get tricky. First, you want to avoid a second pattern that competes with the importance of the main event. Coordinates need to assist and strengthen, not steal attention. That said, you want there to be a natural hierarchy in the flow of design. If you have an oversized floral on the walls, it's fine to select a mini print for pillows. But soften the gap with another pattern that's classified as "medium scale." The same is true with color. Graphic and clean painting with two different colors is one way of designing, but if you prefer a look that has a gradual movement among elements, choose a shade that's in the middle to deliver a stair-step approach to the theme. Both are examples of layering.

Nature manages to sneak its way into so many design schemes. Here, tropical plants and trees complement the garden treillage that gives dimension to the walls.

ABOVE *A soothing palette makes a mix of patterns work without being too busy.*

RIGHT *A bedroom is both the first and last glance of a day. Hues in medium values add a little energy to this restful color scheme.*

As you select main events and go-withs, remember that not everything needs to match. When design appears too perfect, it can look contrived. You'll need an outlier element. If you don't know where to start, take a stroll around your home. I'll bet that you can shop it without having to leave the house. Find something that lives elsewhere and introduce it into the room you are working on. Maybe that's a throw blanket in disparate color. It could also be an antique or needlepoint pillow that has nothing to do with the room. That's what layers you into the room.

If you do prefer a matching look, contrast it with the furniture color. Blue-and-white anything always causes me to at least take a look. Add chi-

one overhead light, which cast light in a place where you didn't necessarily want it. Now lighting is more zone specific. I want a lamp, either a table or a floor lamp, right next to me when I'm sitting in case I want to read. Can lights, even though they are utilitarian, are necessary kitchen and bathroom staples.

Before searching for lighting, make a list of your lighting needs. If your room has no or little art presence, think about a dynamic oversized fixture that also serves as sculpture. It could be a traditional crystal chandelier or a giant modern orb. If you do have artwork in the room, how lovely would it be to cast an extra glow around the piece with either a downlight or a pair of sconces installed on either side of it? High ceilings are a wonderful bonus, but if you have eight-foot

> *When design appears too perfect, it can look contrived. You'll need an outlier element.*

noiserie to it, and I'm hooked. If you like a delicate motif like chinoiserie or toile, I suggest you outfit the room with brown furniture, especially if the furniture forms, too, are delicate. Brown furniture opposes the look with heft and warmth. This is an example of layering through depth.

Regarding go-with patterns, mix the strong lines of geometric motifs with the relaxed forms of florals. Plaids are linear and offer structure. Throw the scheme in the opposite direction with an animal print in a fashionable color or solid-colored pillows that are piped and monogrammed in a coordinating color.

LIGHTING: BRIGHT IDEAS IN LAYERING

Since the beginning of my career, lighting has grown exponentially. Instead of only serving as a useful necessity, it has become a beacon of style.

The functional part of lighting has one purpose, and that's to help us see. That's a lot to consider. I remember the days when lighting meant

ceilings, not to worry. Look at flush-mount fixtures to add a pop of panache. When it comes to pendant lights, they can be installed to all hang at the same height. Hanging them in a cluster at varying heights creates a custom look and loads of intrigue.

Lighting inherently encourages layering, because a room needs to maintain its function in all its areas. Think about buying at least one pair of matching lamps. They can target the design principle of balance in addition to providing light. Lamps of varying heights are fine, depending on where they will be used. If you have the challenge of illuminating a built-in unit, think about a mini lamp that can rest on a shelf, or a sconce or two that are installed on the frame of the unit.

I always recommend putting lights on dimmers. Changing the intensity of the brightness can alter the mood of a room.

Finally, lighting doesn't always reference the electrified kind. Natural daylight enters as a major player in design; during daytime hours, how sunlight pours through windows must be considered.

Lampshades: A New Attitude

For some reason, there always seem to be certain parts of design that are temporarily forgotten and live dormant until there's a resurgence. Such has been the case for lampshades in recent years. History reminds us that lampshades were once anything but low-key. They were silk, pleated, and finished with trims that mimicked a beautifully decorated cake. At some point, though, that decadent level of decoration faded and, for the most part, lampshades were ivory, parchment color, or black. Little variation existed. The good news is there's a new batch of decorative lampshades on the market. Once again, the lampshade is as important as its base. Especially if you have classic, solid-colored ceramic lamps, think about adding a pattern on its shade. Another option is to add decorative trim to a solid-colored shade. A barley shaped, candlestick-style lamp would welcome a punch of color with a lampshade done in a mini print. Materials matter, too. A leather shade would be an ideal moment of luxury in a library or bar. A natural material like raffia or rattan emphasizes the beach look in a seaside location. A glass lampshade adds a glossy finish. Give yourself a break, too. Sometimes a basic lampshade is in fact best, but when you want to up your layering game, think about a shade that's special.

ABOVE *Lampshades are another opportunity to add color and pattern, especially in spaces with lots of solid elements.*

OPPOSITE *Consider your sight line and remember that if you can see artwork at eye level, you likely can't see the flooring, too. This landing space blends a serene palette anchored by the pale floral wallcovering and punctuated with soft color on artwork and on a zigzag rug.*

GROUND RULES:
LAYERING ON THE FLOOR

Much like lighting, flooring is completely functional. It needs to be level and adhere to specific surfaces in specific areas of the home. For example, tile or vinyl is best in a bathroom, where the probability of splashed water at some point will be an issue. Once you have chosen a material, it's time to think about layering.

Generally speaking, the popularity of wall-to-wall carpet has evaporated. Modern-day design encourages hard floor surfaces: either wood, vinyl, or tile. Oftentimes, the choice is made not only for its looks, but for its practicality. A hard surface can be cleaned easily and doesn't trap dust, a common criticism of carpeting, which can make life challenging for sufferers of allergies. But hard surfaces can be cold and echoing. Adding a rug makes a room softer and controls acoustics by absorbing sound.

Always think about rolling out a rug in every room. Remember, rug selection is regularly the starting point of a room's color scheme. For spaces like living rooms or family rooms, I prefer wool rugs. Whether it's subtle and tonal or full of lively pattern, your rug layers color, texture, and warmth.

Sisal and sea grass are other possibilities for rugs. Bind them in a border for definition. In the kitchen, think about gel mats laid on the floor in your work areas. They are available in many looks and can provide soothing cushions that your feet will appreciate while you are preparing meals. Outdoor areas deserve a rug, too, and a plethora of indoor-outdoor materials make boosting the environment outside with style possible.

OPPOSITE *A black faux bamboo chair helps modernize a classic desk.*

RIGHT *An unexpected material lends personality to a room: Although wicker is found typically in sunrooms, here, a wicker slipper chair lightens the sweetness of a pink bedroom.*

SMALL CANVAS, BIG IMPACT

The intimidating parts of design tend to be the big elements: architecture first, and then flooring, cabinetry, wall color, and key furniture pieces. Once we have those in place, however, it's important to continue the design energy on smaller stages. These are spots where styling comes into play. Small accessories serve as the central characters and can move around. The good news is these canvases are never permanent. Every object can stay or go, so there's never really a costly mistake that can be made.

Although I can't make a complete decorative overhaul every year, the mini makeover is something that I can address on a regular basis. In my own home, I'm always reassessing the following: bookshelves, cocktail and console tables, bathroom shelves, the kitchen island, and its backsplash.

The bed is another spot where you can eas-ily make over the look of a room. I will warn you, though, bedding can get costly if you want the luxurious feel of sheets with high thread counts. Also, if you want a custom duvet cover that's fabricated out of a decorative fabric instead of a cover made of sheeting, it will require several yards of fabric. None of this is to scare you or lead you in a different direction, just to provide you with an informed background. Of course, there are ways to achieve great design at every price point. Sheets in color or patterns with beautiful embroidery or appliqué, plus pillows and blankets, can present a layered look that gives the room its voice. On the other hand, some people prefer to create the hotel experience of all-white linens, and that's fine, too. In that case, consider a simple monogram to personalize the bed ensemble.

Perhaps, my favorite small spot to layer is

An effective way to temper daring hues, like this bold red, is to layer neutral tones and natural textures with them.

Traditional palettes turn heads when they are delivered with a breath of fresh air; a Christmas table with gold, green, and red accents is styled atop a floral cloth with unconventional gray and brown tones.

the dining table. An avid entertainer, I get much joy in setting a table for the people I care about. What especially attracts me to crafting a tablescape is the ability to mix old and new, high and low, so easily. Also, by changing centerpieces from flowers on one occasion to collectibles on another, I can set a table without ever repeating.

Because I find so much inspiration from textiles, I always drape my table with a cloth. It's an opportunity to use a fabric that I might not want to live with every day. I've been adding to my arsenal of entertaining accoutrements for years, and it now includes everything from new linens with our monogram, to the porcelain china that we received for our wedding, to vintage cabbage plates that I search for online late at night. To add a natural element to the mix, I advise buying either place mats or chargers in raffia or wicker, too. They can tone down formality, if that's not what you are after.

Here's the best part about a tablescape that other places in the home do not offer in the same manner. A table setting repeats itself several times over. If you are using your table as a laboratory for pairing patterns and color, you can put several exclamation points on your selections, the validation that a setting's repetition shows that the scheme is purposeful and stylish for a reason. So experiment, have fun, and know that however you set your table will elicit gratitude from guests and present a beautiful environment to remember to the occasion with.

COVER TO COVER: LAYERING WITH BOOKS

Our relationships with books have certainly shifted since 2000. Digital alternatives for reading, both for learning and for pleasure, mean that we can minimize the volume of bound books we have. That does not mean that we've ditched them completely, though.

I love books. There's something especially warm and inviting about shelves that are filled with my favorite stories and the subjects that I love. Books can provide memories. I think

Soft green in the living room of this old home works well with historical hues and a pop of contrast from the camel ottoman.

it's special to gift a book and sign the inside with a message. Not only does the subject matter between the covers tell something about a person, books are useful, too, in a design scheme.

Books for Decoration
Versus Books for Reading

If you are like me, your reading materials are both physical books and digital ones. There are novels that I prefer in hard copy, and other quick reads that are fine to absorb from my tablet, which allows me to travel and read without extra weight in my carry-on luggage.

Then there are books used for decoration. Besides filling bookcases with books, I'll pull them off the shelves to layer elsewhere throughout the room. Books are great risers. If you want to elevate an object, try setting it on a book or two. It might give you the right height to play with other design elements that are around it. When you have a book on a table, guests will pick it up and flip through, too. Books are conversation starters.

Antique and vintage books also fall into "books for decoration." Allow yourself to buy books that are worn and have texture. The colors of antique and vintage books are usually rich and warm in subdued hues. They look appropriate among special objects that you want to highlight and offer their own version of patina, much like a ceramic or piece of wood. I recommend buying several in the same color for an effective design boost.

ROUGH (AND SMOOTH) AROUND THE EDGES: LAYERING WITH TEXTURE

Texture is an area of design that oftentimes takes a back seat to color and pattern. It's equally important, though, and can be an alternative to color and pattern. When we talk about texture in design, it's common to automatically think of natural materials and their rough feel. Raffia and wicker, sea grass, sisal, jute, and grass cloth are all examples of

ABOVE *I find that collections, even utilitarian ones, can make a sculptural statement when organized with purpose.*

OPPOSITE *A little vintage here and there gives a room soul. I lean on old finds for a bar setup, and often discover unexpected pieces at thrift shops and online auctions.*

ABOVE *Incorporating just a bit of natural material in a room adds instant visual warmth.*

OPPOSITE *Grass-cloth wallpaper makes a stylish backdrop and textural layer in this bedroom.*

materials that are used for furniture, wallcoverings, and rugs. I like to incorporate just a bit of a natural material in a room. It's instant visual warmth. An easy way to layer texture is with a rug.

We are most familiar with wicker and rattan on furniture—*outdoor* furniture. They will always be staples outside, but consider bringing them indoors as well. The materials look right at home in a sun-room that's flooded with daylight. Furniture that is wrapped in linen, raffia, or even parchment delivers a perfectly imperfect aesthetic. These materials plus grass cloth are also suitable for wallcoverings. Wherever you decide to use them, know that natural materials are just that—natural—so it's difficult to go wrong. If nothing else, these materials will inject a dose of warmth, and that's always welcome.

Textures can be smooth, too. In design, think lacquer, glass, metals, Lucite, and high-gloss paint. A high-gloss paint might not be a great option for your walls, but it does make a statement on moldings or built-ins. Also consider making a ceiling shine with high-gloss paint.

Textiles are also where texture makes a stylish mark. Chunky wools, mohair, bouclé, chenille, cable knits, and crewelwork can be used on upholstery and as accents. Leather and hair-on hide extend physical and visual texture. Distressed leather, just like distressed wood, shows a mottled finish that translates into texture and age.

Layering texture is the key to avoiding a look that is too new. It is also the key to layering when color and patterns are intentionally absent.

WHEN ENOUGH IS ENOUGH: THE ART OF STOPPING

Time tends to dictate the level to which one layers. In my career, I've watched design evolve from traditional with lots of objects to clean and edited, then back to a maximalist attitude. There is a point when layering can be too much, so before you invest in too many things, here are a few tips that I've found helpful:

- **Avoid a look that is cluttered by giving purpose to objects.** Every time you add something, reassess how the group looks. I like to occasionally remove a couple of pieces so that my objects can breathe.

Layering texture is the key to avoiding a look that is too new. It is also the key to layering when color and patterns are intentionally absent.

- **Say goodbye for good or for a while.** We all have some holiday decorations but wouldn't dream of living with them all year long. The same is true of nonseasonal things. Give them a break.

- **Embrace simplicity.** Layering doesn't always mean adding objects. It's OK to not flood your space with furniture of all sizes, accessories of all kinds, and a complicated schedule of colors and fabrics. Simple is sometimes best, and although my aesthetic tends to be more involved, a simplified room can read as stunning.

Whether you are new to the layering game or have the confidence to let your imagination fly, remember that the best guide for good design is your own two eyes.

Identify a stylish way to show off books.
Stacking by color adds to the palette story.

chapter 5

UPDATING CLASSICS: DECORATIVE TOUCHES THAT ARE NOW AND FOREVER

ABOVE *Always classic: a console table and a pair of dragon-themed chinoiserie stools.*

ABOVE AND OPPOSITE *Neutral-toned wallcovering provides an active base for displaying artwork.*

PAGE 144 *A classic can span many styles—they are treasures that stand the test of time.*

ur homes can become lessons in history, three-dimensional scrapbooks filled with personal treasures that are meaningful to us. Those treasures that stand the test of time throughout our design journeys are *classics*.

As I first explained in Chapter 1, a classic has staying power. It begins with beautiful design and is something that we return to because of its functionality. A classic can span many styles and represent those moments that consistently provide pleasure to us. This chapter will help define *your* classics and provide ways to update those that need a refresh. In the end, we want our homes to embrace what's old, what's new, and what's been reimagined to deliver a new era of joy.

WHAT AND WHO DEFINES A CLASSIC

Classics emerge from many sources, and chances are you stumble upon them daily while registering what is around you. In the visual world, you might recognize paneling in a library or the grand silhouette of a wing chair. There are classics in other parts of life, too. Think about that beloved song that you've bought in every form of recorded technology since it first hit the radio when you were a child, or the well-fitting blazer that's your fashion go-to with a simple dress or a casual pair of jeans.

History oftentimes defines classics as moments that are common and have proven to be tried and true. Incorporating these stereotypical classics ensures that a design will be built on a recognizable and timeless foundation.

Symmetry in a fresh color scheme can be modern, even when elements lean to the traditional side. Here, blush, peach, and blue tones mix on classic furniture, on a statement fabric, and on abstract art for a soft, calming presentation.

There's a second driving force, however, that determines *personal* classics, and that is *you*. It is your roster of personal classics that imbues not only the looks that you find attractive, but the emotions that provide you with a lovely memory or thought of someone or some time that was special.

HISTORY IN THE BOOKS

The academicians of design inform us of the classic design elements that have appeared and continue to appear in architecture and interiors since their inception. Design enthusiasts like you and me tend to recognize the classic design elements when strolling about: moldings, fluted columns, a crystal chandelier, brass candlesticks, and a Chesterfield sofa, to name a handful among hundreds. These classics may be seen in significant works and have been repeated because of their visual impact, be it bold and grand or understated.

YOUR CLASSICS

When we want to identify classic items that refer to our personal story, our best source is ourselves. We write our own histories, after all. I know that you probably have favorite design elements that follow you no matter where you live. I certainly do. For example, consider shades of blue. Blue and its most common companion, white, is classic in the design world due to its use on china patterns and other ceramics. In nature, it's as classic as the sky and contrasting clouds or the water and its whitecapped waves. The combo is a solid foundation that allows many variations. I've used blue with white for decades; in fact, I am using it to decorate my outdoor furniture scheme. Pillows, ceramics, and a tabletop look divine against the backdrop of my lush gardens.

Not wanting to get stuck in a rut, though, for the last several years I've taken to using blue with *other* companions for an updated shift in my aesthetic world. Most notably, I've become drawn to green. The verdant cousin of blue, green lends a coolness and calming effect that I find dreamy. Green is what I chose for my business logo. I've used green with white to inspire and energize work and creativity in a home office, and I've used it as a teammate to blue in a grand dining room designed to be youthful. I can forecast that no matter where I decide to live, both blue and green will join me, but the color accents that play with them may vary.

Our homes can become lessons in history, three-dimensional scrapbooks filled with personal treasures that are meaningful to us.

You might get out your favorite notepad or productivity app and make a list of your favorite things. If there is something—a piece of furniture, arched doors, a specific color—that you find yourself leaning toward time after time, then it's a classic to you. Remember, there's no right or wrong to your personal decorative preferences. It's how you execute them that makes them successful.

ELEMENTS THAT STAND
THE TEST OF TIME

To me, classics are those heavy hitters that show up often in my work. It's no secret that my aesthetic percolates in bold colors and patterns with lots of texture. My list of classics might look different than someone else's. The following elements show up on *many* lists of design classics, but the weight of each may shift. For the purpose of this book, I want to share my favorites with you and encourage you to use them or adapt them to your liking.

A simple silhouette suits the pattern of a burlwood side table. Velvet sofas add glamorous texture.

TOP *Plaid can sometimes conjure visions of boardrooms and stiff libraries. A plaid in a light, updated color palette can keep the traditional pattern relevant and current.*

BOTTOM *Oftentimes it's color that can make a space appear dated or dazzling. Here, chinoiserie inspires.*

Blue and green brings the outdoors in. Brown-stained wood pieces, including a faux-bamboo bed and an old chest of drawers, add warmth.

*Shades of blue go in and out of fashion:
Choose a current hue for a look that is fresh.
Here, the furnishings, accessories, and trim
repeat the palette of the striped floor.*

Patterns

You will be hard-pressed to find a room that I've designed without patterns. I turn to them to give a room life. Here are some of the ones that I've found most useful.

Chinoiserie

Full of pretty moments, from flowers to birds, chinoiserie is the Western world's interpretation and nod to the facets of design that emerged in China. I long for the moments when I can stretch a floor-to-ceiling mural of a chinoiserie scene on the walls to add a delicate touch to the symmetry that comes from a dining room. I oftentimes accessorize with a display of ceramic tea canisters and ginger jars. Recently, I've even developed an elevated fondness for pagodas, another staple in chinoiserie.

Plaids, Checks, and Stripes

If there is one group of patterns that conjures vivid pictures of decorative history, it's plaids, checks, and stripes. Images of wood-paneled libraries and dens in a rich, dark palette come to mind. That way of decorating is old-school and serious, though. I like the challenge of taking the pieces of a scenario like that, which can be stuck in time, and making them relevant again.

Plaids

Don't feel that the linear grid of plaids will keep you stuck in a box. When I'm addressing color schemes, one trick that works for me is lightening the scheme. Swap dark jewel tones of dated plaids with light pastels or hues with medium values that infuse the space with light and current color. Especially in a library that doubles as an office, you'll probably want your surroundings to be inspiring and spirited. Another tip that I find useful when modernizing a classic on a fabric or wallpaper is to pick an oversized version of it. Finally, you might take a plaid away from a traditional armchair or wallcovering and apply it to an unexpected spot. Think about a floor tile in the bathroom or on a modern slipper chair.

OPPOSITE *Checks pair with many patterns. Here, checked shades balance the novelty star motif on the walls.*

RIGHT *Block print florals add an artisanal touch. This toss pillow brings saturated but subdued tones into the scheme.*

Checks

If you are like me, checks conjure images of happy times. In the summer, we've probably all been seated around a picnic table on occasion, where a checked cloth is laid to provide a cheerful base for a bevy of fresh vegetable salads and plates of sliced watermelon. In my world of fashion, I'm known to host a summer gathering in a ruffled or tiered dress made of a checked fabric, which I always think of as a classic. If you look at the other end of the calendar, checks are a staple come Christmastime, when checked ribbons finish packages with lavish bows, or buffalo checks wrap giant mugs waiting to steam with hot chocolate.

What I like about a check is its versatility. It can be a primary pattern or used as a quiet and simple go-with to support another motif. For a graphic look, emphasize checks by choosing a check with contrasting colors. Tonal variations in color will soften the geometric qualities.

Stripes

Stripes can be confining, but good news: They don't have to be. With stripes, it's not color combinations that send them into the history books as much as the forms themselves. However, there are lots of occasions that call for a strong linear silhouette. Today's inventory of patterns has loosened its reins on stripes, fortunately. When the situation calls for a relaxing environment, think about choosing a stripe with flowing lines that are unbridled and provide an organic look.

Floral Patterns

Floral patterns are impossible to ignore and something that we *want* to love. They represent nature, the outdoors, and beauty. It makes sense, then, to welcome them into the home, but oftentimes floral patterns can be not only intimidating, but dated. The scare factor emerges from their feminine qualities, which can read as *too sweet* if florals are not controlled and applied with thoughtful and careful placement.

There are a few rules of thumb that I've discovered over the years to help me navigate the thousands of floral patterns that are available. If you struggle with knowing when to use a floral pattern and which one to select, keep the following in mind:

Go big

An oversized version of a flower takes it away from the field and the garden and into the world of art. Using a flower that's been blown up on a fabric or wallcovering finds beauty in its singular, basic form. It's a graphic presentation, and

When I'm addressing color schemes, one trick that works for me is lightening the scheme.

graphic usually results in a clean and modern appearance. Here's another little tip that we find useful when addressing a small room: An oversized floral pattern can visually extend the height of a space. To make a bold statement, use it on the wall or on straight-paneled window treatments.

Think simple

Flowers can be complicated, with lots of delicate petals, leaves, and stems. Since I'm a lover of patterns, florals crop up often in my designs. One artistic technique that especially draws me to floral patterns is the Indian block print. I appreciate that in this technique the forms are not too perfect. The flowers are artists' interpretations through a cultured and worldly lens. One of my favorite ways to use an Indian block print is when I entertain. I'll drape a textile over a table, then add all the entertaining accoutrements. There is always joyful color inspiration and a casual attitude that comes from this textile, which is typically manufactured in cotton. Although the forms on block prints can be small and dainty, there's something about their imperfections that alludes to history and an artisanal hand.

Precious Paneling: Millwork

It seems a shame to remove paneling and moldings from a room. Before you grab the pry bar, head to the home improvement center for a look at paint that will usher the molding into contemporary design. In an old library or den, where wood paneling might cover the room floor to ceiling, choose a neutral that will complement that wood in a fashionable scheme. If you are a little more daring, pick a light to medium color—a shade of blue, for instance—to create a blue room. Bathe the wood paneling entirely in that color, which will provide a solid foundation. A solid-colored room, regardless of color, gives license for additional solid-colored accents or, better yet in my eyes, a pattern.

If you can't bear the thought of painting wood, take a look at the new stains that exist. Strip cherry red or yellow honey tones that were on-trend in decades past. You might be drawn to the handsome dark gray and black stains that, even in their undiluted states, allow the wood grain to show through. If you prefer a light treatment, think about a limed stain that delivers a raw and natural look.

The addition of classic millwork can sometimes be enough to add depth and interest to an area. Consider leaving it without additional decoration in spots that need a little visual relief.

Dining rooms are meant to dazzle, especially since they are often used at night. Here, the dining chairs pop in a strong teal that echoes the ceiling.

ABOVE *Flowers seem to give a cheerful outlook to all spaces. An unbridled wallpaper pattern gives way to a fresh floral bouquet.*

OPPOSITE *Oversized patterns make ideal choices for instances that require significant yardage, like window panels that will show a full repeat.*

Make accessories matter

One reason that floral patterns can be intimidating is that there is oftentimes an overload of them. There's no need to re-create your exterior garden inside. Instead, you might invite floral *accessories* to the space. They can be more easily controlled and removed. Throw pillows are an ideal decorating tool when an additional textile is needed. A table skirt can hint at florals without being overwhelming.

Then there are ceramics. Buy a vase that's all white or all black with sculptural flowers that add to the form's silhouette instead of being painted onto the vase. Or use floral plates in an updated way. One way to modernize the look of antique floral plates on a wall is to create an organic layout for the plates. Pick a spot on the wall where lots of plates are grouped together, then loosen the layout as the group grows outward. This is a great way to give a fresh outlook to a collection of heirlooms or flea market finds that you've picked up.

Find style in minis

There are instances that call for a small and delicate pattern. If that's what you love, I say, "Go for it." That brings me to ditzy prints. These small-scale prints don't have to be florals, but they commonly are. Many manufacturers produce ditzy prints, but there's no maker of this pattern type that is more classic than Liberty of London, a British emporium of upscale goods for the home that also has its own textile collection. Liberty of London is famous for its no-apology outlook on floral patterns. I like a ditzy print because, while there are usually loads of colors represented, from a distance the pattern's small-scale delivery reads almost as a solid. Consider incorporating a miniature floral pattern into a guest room. Wrap the room in the pattern, applying it to all walls, and use a matching fabric to make the window treatment and bed linens. It's a win-win treatment. You won't have to live with the pattern every day, and your guests will love the dynamic design for a short-term stay.

COLORS AND FINISHES

Every year, the new "in" color is revealed. This may be a bit too frequently for the home furnishings world. It's a strategic marketing tactic, but it does push a regular rethink of what colors we love. Here are my takes on colors that I assign to the "classics" category.

Black

Old interior design books dictate that it's necessary to display something black in every space. It's my opinion that there is plenty of opportunity for design success even without it, but a dark piece does have its purpose. Black adds weight and can keep elements from the appearance of floating in rooms with tall or vaulted ceilings.

LEFT AND OPPOSITE
Outdoor spaces are ideal for seasonal decorations.

If you are going to incorporate black into a space that is otherwise light or colorful, make sure that what you choose has presence so that it doesn't read like an afterthought. For instance, contrast an all-white kitchen with an island that is painted black. Gather a collection of black objects and show them off in a built-in cabinet for a dynamic art display. One tip to remember: Don't take the direction to use something black too literally. Soften the color if necessary. For upholstery, instead of solid black, using a tweed or bouclé can temper the dark neutral with coordinating threads.

Blue and Green

While I use blue frequently throughout my interiors, my update on this color favorite is to choose another color as my favorite altogether. I lean to green as my favorite color as an alternative to blue. Also, I don't disregard those hues that exist between blue and green. Turquoise, aqua, and teal steal their values from the tropics and can put a fresh spin on traditional blue. I'm especially fond of these hues when I want to inject a youthful presence.

If you know that you love blue but want a look that departs completely from anything historical, start by selecting a new shade of this favorite. When you do have vintage and antique pieces, display them differently.

Brown

Let me be specific: I'm talking about brown wood. For over a decade, wood in a brown stain, whether it was as paneling, molding, or furniture, was not in fashion. In its place was painted wood, architecturally in white and on furniture, in any color of the spectrum. It's my opinion that what dated the wood pieces was the stains, so it's worth a revisit now with current tones.

Brown wood is an example of the fact that *classic* doesn't always mean *current*. I'm excited about bird's-eye maple and burl right now. Both are lovely materials, but ones that have gone through periods when they weren't popular.

ABOVE *Classics are capable of being modern; it's all about the styling. A black-patterned backdrop gives an edgy foundation to a Louis-style chair with a caned back and a spot table made sleek in glossy red lacquer.*

OPPOSITE *A glamorous moment is a welcome addition in a dark room. A mirrored desk flickers light throughout this room.*

Try green and blue in unexpected places, such as an angled ceiling that becomes graphic hovering over solid-colored flooring.

ABOVE *Traditional ceramic accessories from tea canisters to ginger jars to statement pagodas lend a joyful touch in current, fashionable colors.*

OPPOSITE *Accents are design elements that can really alter the mood of a space. Blue notes in the artwork, lighting, and bed linens support the cool tone of the green headboard.*

Turning Treasures into Artwork

When we think about artwork, we tend to imagine traditional works done in oils or watercolors. When it comes to framing, though, original artwork is not required. The wall is an ideal place to keep history alive with mementos from those life events that were important in to you, so as you are contemplating how to fill a wall space, dive into your scrapbooks and boxes to see if there is something worthy of decorative presence. Here are some ideas about what to take to your local framer to create a special piece of artwork:

• Tickets or programs from live performances, sporting competitions, or concerts. Plastic hotel room keys: Make sure that you always ask the hotel where you are staying if you can take home your plastic key. If the key represents a special trip or hotel, framing it to hang on the wall will always keep the trip top of mind.

• Fallen leaves gathered during a vacation, then pressed. Preserve their fiery color with an acrylic paint medium. You could also finish them with gold or silver leaf for a layer of sheen.

• A favorite garment from childhood, such as a christening gown or a first day of kindergarten shirt. Children's swimsuits or trunks are fun when framed for decorating a lake or beach house.

Objects of the same color en masse add presence. For small-scale objects such as candlesticks, a collection of mismatched forms appear collected over time.

OPPOSITE *The pair of ceramic lamps atop a sideboard with sleek wood door fronts is oversized to draw attention to the grand area. Brass hardware introduces sparkle.*

Likewise, oak is widely used for its abundance and accessibility. But like me, you can probably remember a time a few decades back when oak's color and application were not so appealing. Reimagined in new finishes, oak has regained style status.

THE ART OF SMALLS: WEAVING HISTORY INTO YOUR HOME

Telling a story through objects is a visual lesson in time. The story doesn't have to be your own, though. Perusing vintage and antiques shops and fairs, flea markets, and consignment shops has become design enthusiasts' national pastime. I not only find it personally enjoyable, but, as a designer, see it as a part of sourcing that's important to make projects unique.

As you shop for your home, think about how you might take something that is old and has been loved by someone else and make it your own. It can be an heirloom from someone who has played a special role in your life. It could also be a piece from a stranger that makes you wonder about the piece's story. Either way, touches of history contribute to a home's layering.

However, even with years of design experience, there are times when I am indecisive about buying a piece. Vintage finds can be tricky, but if you start small and simple, you'll get the hang of sourcing these treasures. Here are some guidelines that I use when I am buying.

Identify Value

Set a number that is your price limit ahead of time. If a piece is being sold at a high price, you may need to do some additional research to see if it is rare, has special markings, or has any other justification that warrants top dollar. For small objects that are reasonably priced, buy what you love.

Collect in Multiples

To make a statement, look for something that you can buy in multiples or collect over time. A collection will create a strong impact. For instance,

blue-and-white ceramics and ironstone are plentiful. Depression glass is, too. If you like something that's a tad more rustic, look for boxes, bowls, and trays that have a finish that is chipped or worn. Then there are books. Old books can soften bookshelves with their cloth covers, usually in neutral colors. (See Chapter 4 for more details about collecting books.) The point is: Find something relatively inexpensive and buy lots of them. It will give your room a look that is truly one of a kind.

Think About Alterations

As you think about old pieces, remember this: Not everything old is good or worth keeping in its original state. So if you want to paint a chair with great shape, do it. Reupholster it with updated fabric and repaint the frame with a glossy lacquer finish. Here's an idea that I've used time and time again to update an object that's going to rest on a table. Secure it to an acrylic base. The sleek, modern presentation of clear acrylic gives a piece of vintage Murano glass, an architectural fragment,

LEFT *Shying away from traditional classic design for fear that it will become stodgy is the wrong idea. Find updated versions of classics and create a mood board to check the vibe and energy of the selections.*

OPPOSITE *I always find that the addition of natural shades tempers the formality of a space full of varying patterns.*

or anything small more prominence. The old-new execution says that something with history can exist beautifully in the present.

Adding acrylic is an example of modernizing. You can also personalize something, as I did to the étagère with fretwork sides that I inherited from my grandmother. In its original state it was stained wood, but I tend to be attracted to color and the lightness that paint offers. I had it painted in white lacquer. Now the piece represents my grandmother's style and mine. In its new iteration, I'm more likely to use it because it's more me. For your own inherited items, you pay a tribute when you keep a piece. Take the opportunity to write a new chapter for it with your own spin.

The desk is antique, and its ornate detail allows for styling with only a few objects. When you score a prominent old piece like this one, don't over-style. Its age and patina will deliver plenty of interest.

HISTORY WITH A FACELIFT

One of the job requirements that I look forward to most is the hunt for new products. Whether I'm flipping through the catalog of a new vendor that has been sent to me, strolling the aisles at a trade fair, or shopping for myself, there's a thrill in the discovery of something new. Right now, I'm especially attracted to new versions of what has been done before, especially from a color perspective.

Ceramics, especially classics such as ginger jars and tea canisters, are a design staple in my work, and are typically found in blue-and-white. I've discovered, however, that for a fresh take on something so classic, a simple shift in color can make "basic" take a breath of contemporary air and delight with a happy and fresh spirit. I've found examples of both of these ceramic forms in pink and white, green and white, even in a neutral khaki at times. Using these classics in a new color nods to the past but shows that design is ever-evolving.

Another example of updates on classics has to do with certain materials from what are now considered endangered or threatened animals. New accessories reproducing their natural pat-

Ceramics are a design staple in my work, and are typically found in blue and white.

terns and colors have been made with synthetic materials. Resin is oftentimes used to create goods such as boxes and trays that mimic the aesthetics of the originals. This is the perfect opportunity to update your look, imitating an old-school material. Select a piece with clean lines so it's clear that you have married old with new in your room's design. Boxes and trays are ideal, because they are functional and can be used to store TV remotes, keys, sunglasses, and anything else that needs to be disguised.

The time-honored skills of our grandmothers are resurging on the design scene, although fewer people have been taught to do them nowadays. Think about needlepoint and quilting. It's oftentimes not the craft itself that is dated, rather its presentation. Needlepoint is not only enjoying renewed interest for its aesthetics, it also has become popular among hobbyists who want to be creative. Needlepoint canvases in trendy prints and with cheeky phrases are being stitched into pillows, inserts for acrylic trays, and game boards for chess or backgammon. Are you looking for something to keep your hands busy while you relax at the lake or in front of the fire on a cold, windy night? Make a visit to your local needlepoint shop. Chances are you will find a modern canvas that speaks to you far more than one with a dated bundle of flowers that recalls your childhood.

For quilting, pattern and color choice can take this classic art form and push it into modern-day design easily. Many old quilts don geometric motifs. If you love the idea of a quilt and are considering having one made, pick colors that will form an ombré effect instead of a traditional repetitive design.

When it comes to updating classics, make sure that you don't over-update. There's a fine line between ushering classics into a current era and altering them so much that they no longer qualify as classics. The tried and true exist because they've stood the test of time, and their continual use keeps them from merely defining one moment.

That said, classics come and go, achieving popularity for a couple of years and then fading into the history books for a while. When this happens, put your classics away and allow them to reappear when the time is right. What's most important, though, is your perspective on classics. Identify what's important to you, what makes you feel comfortable, and find those familiar items that bring you joy. Write your decorative history with looks that *you* love.

chapter 6

TURNING PRACTICAL INTO STUNNING

ABOVE *Chances are, shelves are needed somewhere in your home. The appearance of built-in shelves can be elevated with decorative extras such as a patterned wallpaper that is applied to the wall behind them.*

OPPOSITE *I believe spaces should inspire our duties and undertakings with style.*

PAGE 178 *A masculine palette doesn't have to be dark. Use medium-toned blue and pair it with sand, camel, and light brown.*

A phrase I first learned at college in an architectural history class has stuck with me ever since. It didn't take years practicing in this field for me to understand the power of the three words, which have guided us designers, architects, and manufacturers for more than a century: Form follows function.

The phrase, proclaimed by esteemed American architect Louis Sullivan, is a learning tool that anyone who revels in design can apply. In fact, they are words that I keep in mind in every room that I create. Of course, we all want our task-driven rooms to function. Isn't it even better, though, when our spaces can inspire our duties and undertakings with style?

This chapter demonstrates how rooms that are typically hardworking spaces can delight and be beautiful, too. Surroundings matter to us

all, and since life's operating tasks are usually non-negotiables, we can make sure that they are always completed while we are hugged by moments of visual charm.

PRODUCTS OF THEIR TIME

If we look back at the environments that we've lived in over several decades, we see that design was oftentimes a product of what was available at that time. To explore this further, I've broken down the history of practical spaces into two categories: purpose and technology.

Purpose

There was a time when a room had a one-track mind. At first, kitchens were solely for cooking; later they were for eating in as well. Bathrooms were for personal care. Laundry rooms were vis-

Visually it's easier to locate items and use what you have if things are not cluttered together.

ited maybe once or twice a week to wash and fold clothes, and often were located in the basement, far away from where the clothes lived. Simple, focused tasks were all that mattered, and the truth is that, at the time, that use worked and was enough.

Today, though, that single-purpose function mindset is archaic. When I'm assessing a space, whether it's the blank slate of a new-build or an existing one that needs an updated scheme, I not only consider what job it's intended to do, but also what else it can possibly be for. I'm sure you've had the same thoughts in your own home, rethinking flow and efficiency here and there.

One key factor that has shifted the function of the public spaces in our homes is work on the home computer and related devices. Join me for a trip down memory lane to life-before-Internet homework situations. To study for a test or write a book report, did you sit at the desk in your bed-

room like I did until everything was complete? A computer with Internet access didn't emerge until the 1990s. We all know how the Internet has altered our thoughts regarding computer time. Most important, if there are children and teenagers in the house, I'm guessing that, like me, you want to monitor their online activity. That means assigning an area in the open where devices—from computers to tablets, even game systems—can be used with safety measures in place.

Technology

Most of us feel the excitement that comes with new technology. We've all been there. The allure probably starts at an early age, for reasons that seem so trivial now. I remember how thrilled I was as a child when the sitcoms of my 1980s youth could be recorded, so I could see them later in the event that a school activity interfered with their airtime. When I was an adult, music experienced a pivotal moment, too, when the iPod made its debut in 2001. All of a sudden, my life's soundtrack and that of the generations before and after me were available at my fingertips, all at the same time.

In the design world, technology isn't necessarily about entertainment, rather about efficiency and practicality. Especially in the kitchen arena, technology drives design. Take a look at appliances, for example. Offerings such as cooling or heating drawers can change kitchen organization and free up refrigerator space. Speaking of refrigerators, would you consider a smart one? Buying a model that tells you when you are running low on milk may seem like an unnecessary extravagance, until it saves you a return trip to the market and, consequently, time. Even though I have a general formula to help homeowners establish structure and organization in their own lives, I am always looking to improve and find new ways to tackle challenges, especially those that involve our use of time.

OPPOSITE *Rooms that are intended to spark creativity should be creative. An active wallpaper is a sure way to charge a craft room with inspiration.*

A mudroom can be a first glimpse into what's to come throughout the remainder of the house. Commit to giving it style. A bench with attractive cushioning and glamorous mirrored closet doors prove that functional spaces don't have to sacrifice aesthetics.

A kitchen palette of contrasting neutrals offers depth and warmth.

FOCUS ON THE FUTURE

We may be able to forecast what's on the immediate horizon, but it's impossible to know what design will deliver ten years from now. I do have tips, though, that we can all consider to keep our task-driven rooms useful but modern and stylish, too. Nobody wants a short expiration date on either the technology or the decorative scheme of their home, and there many spots where you can add dynamic touches that have staying power.

Integrate Appliances

When you can, I suggest integrating kitchen appliances so that their finishes are concealed by panels made to match your cabinetry. Finishes then become a nonissue. That said, stainless steel is classic, so if you like the look of it, show it off. Since it's unlikely that you will overhaul your kitchen cabinetry as often as you upgrade an appliance, keeping the appliance covered buys you time and keeps your look current and cohesive.

Let Space Breathe

When you've outfitted an area with new built-ins, cabinets, and shelving, it's tempting to load them up, but I'm advising that you don't stuff them full. Leave a comfortable amount of space empty to adapt to situations and needs that you might have later. Visually it's also easier to locate items and use what you have if things are not cluttered together. After a trip to Italy or some other culinary-savvy destination, you may decide to buy a small appliance that will aid your cooking of that country's food, so leave some room.

Avoid Trends

If there's a trend that's grabbing your attention, keep in mind that there are several places where you can introduce it when it's hot and usher it out when it's not. Make sure you're not opting for the trendy choice for the more expensive or difficult-to-change elements. Paint colors can be altered easily enough, but choose countertops, for instance, with purpose. Pick a surface that you truly love, not one that every house on the street ordered because it was posted again and again on social media. The same is true regarding flooring. Replacing flooring is another costly change, so choose something classic, or commit to a look that's based on your personal taste and not on a publicized movement. When you want to add a bit of a look that's of the moment, do it with towels, both kitchen and bath, dinnerware, and even lighting.

A GUIDE TO CREATING FUNCTIONAL SPACES

There are two research activities that need to happen for success in creating a functional space: asking questions and making lists. Don't be scared by the "homework" part. I find that a favorite notepad and a steaming cup of my favorite coffee or glass of wine after hours makes the process fun.

We rank certain rooms higher than others. Spaces that we intend to be high-functioning require extra thought and consideration. Attention to detail makes sure that the rooms will aid the way we use and live in them. For each room, ask yourself a few key questions:

- How is this space currently used?
- How do we want the space to be used?
- Does it make sense to remodel, or will cosmetic changes suffice?

Keep a Log

I find the best way to cover all uses of a space is to keep a log of activities done in the space over a couple of weeks, because otherwise there's a good chance that you'll miss things. Even I sometimes omit an activity in certain spaces. This log may lead to discoveries and questions. For instance, if you are a frequent traveler and are regularly filling your luggage in your closet or bedroom, should you have an island or packing station where you can organize your travel needs before adding them to a suitcase? Does your mudroom serve not only the humans in your house but the furry members of the family, too?

TOP LEFT *The walls in this mudroom are loaded with cabinets. An arresting floor tile fills the space with both pattern and additional color. The under-cabinet pet-feeding area is unique and something fun to try in a utilitarian space.*

BOTTOM LEFT *A place for everything helps maintain organization. Invest in drawer inserts, which will keep contents divided and easy to spot.*

TOP RIGHT *Layering textures in a hardworking room brings a joyful mood to mundane tasks. Comfortable seating encourages a moment of rest.*

BOTTOM RIGHT *A blank wall in a functional space is a missed opportunity. Think about its potential for additional seating, storage, and hooks. This mudroom accomplishes all three.*

Then ample storage for extra pet treats, food and water bowls, and leashes are all important elements that should be listed when you are thinking about storage.

Make Lists

I always look forward to this part of the design process with the homeowners I'm helping. When you begin the design process, I suggest scrolling through social media to see what you like; then if you can, visit a local showroom or two to see workstations and organization and storage ideas in person. I've spent plenty of nights pinning clever ideas that I happen upon to my digital boards.

Making lists will also clarify what you don't want or don't need. Refrigerated wine storage, for instance, has made its way into many kitchens. However, if you're not a frequent wine drinker or entertainer, it doesn't make sense to waste space on this.

There are so many ways to corral design ideas, from tear sheets to digital boards, but once you have those, keep a list. Just like the rooms that we plan to be multipurpose, lists are reminders, organizers, and editors all at the same time.

Different rooms have different functions, of course. I want to share considerations that I find useful when I'm contemplating these spaces, both for myself and for homeowners. Additionally, I love to chat about those spots that welcome decorative touches so that the design is personal.

KITCHENS

If I were in a room with everyone who is reading this, I'd ask for a show of hands of those whose kitchen is the heart of the home. I'm guessing that it would be close to 100 percent.

What is it about the kitchen that draws people together? It's my opinion that the kitchen's multisensory experience delivers all that makes us feel good and welcome. There are wonderful aromas and flavors. Both of those are why the kitchen exists. If you are having people over, you are probably playing soft music in the background. Tactile moments, from rush seating on breakfast nook chairs to the smooth surface of a marble-top island, are worth running your fingertips against to feel. Finally, the collective visual statement of hard and soft surfaces, shiny finishes, and forms specific to kitchens makes this space a treat in more than one way.

Organizing all your dry goods, snacks, and paper goods vertically allows them to be seen easily.

As I take you through each functional space throughout the kitchen perhaps you will identify specific components to study and think about, and learn how to make them aesthetically impactful as well as functional.

The Pantry

What you use as your pantry space affects how the rest of your kitchen functions. I always opt for a walk-in pantry if space allows. Organizing all your dry goods, snacks, and paper goods vertically allows them to be seen easily. Plus, pantries are an ideal spot to house small appliances and larger serveware such as platters so they are not in the way when they are not being used.

Cabinetry

You'll need to decide what types of things your cabinetry will need to house. Pots and pans can be set into drawers or pull-out shelves, but they can hang from a rack, too, for a dynamic visual statement. You might be noticing a lot of open shelving these days. It can look great, especially when stacked with dinnerware of all the same color. Just keep in mind, open shelving means that all that rests on it is exposed to dust. If the upkeep is not a concern, then go for it.

OPPOSITE *Scheming a plan for pantries so all the pantry contents are organized lends visual order and adds to the functionality.*

ABOVE *Lighting is the key to adding dazzle to a bar space. Choose pendants with personality and a bit of sparkl.*

OPPOSITE *An all-white kitchen is a blank slate for just about any accent that you can dream up. The range can be subtle with tonal, textured tile, or glamorous with luxurious contrasting brass.*

Countertops for Food Preparation

Picking a counter surface arguably requires more confidence than choosing any other kitchen detail, in part because of expense. Regardless of the material that you select, a countertop, simply put, provides a flat surface for food preparation. I prefer the organic look of a natural material such as marble or quartzite. I also specify quartz frequently, as it comes in myriad colors and is extremely durable. How likely are you to clean up spills right away? Take note that those white marble beauties that are the crown jewels of so many of today's kitchens aren't so compatible with spilled red wine or smudged beets. If you

Flip through performance-grade fabric swatch books and find fabrics that will be easy to clean in case of spills.

know that you may not get to clean up a spill right away, white marble might not be the wisest choice. On the other hand, if baking is your passion, the cool surface temperature of a natural material like marble makes rolling dough a cinch.

Eating Areas

For so long it seemed as if every kitchen that I worked on needed both a breakfast area and island space with plenty of seating. Many families still want both, but if you find that everyone in your house only wants to sit at the island, forgo the breakfast nook—or vice versa. Take note that, in order to function, a room needs to address *your* needs right now and in the foreseeable future, not those of another family who may live in the house someday.

There is an explosion of available performance fabrics on the market, which are regularly marketed for households with kids and pets. But I ask: Why not choose a performance fabric on kitchen seating? There's no shortage of patterns or

textures. Flip through performance-grade fabric swatch books and find fabrics that will be easy to clean in case of spills. If you like the idea of a banquette, ask yourself whether or not you still need a couple of single chairs for anyone who may have challenges scooting in and out of banquette seating.

Eating Counters and Barstools

How high do you want to sit and for how long? That will determine if you want counter-height (a seat that is 24 to 26 inches/61 to 66 cm high) or bar-height (a seat that is 28 to 30 inches/71 to 76 cm high) stools when building from scratch or renovating. Stools can be sculptural, with slim profiles, or fully upholstered with tall backs for support. During the pandemic, a number of people found themselves using their kitchen island as a makeshift office. If your stools will be used for more than just a meal, consider an upholstered model that will support a longer sit. Whether stools are upholstered or not, their forms are important. After all, you will have more than one stool, so its silhouette on repeat will make a statement.

Task and Decorative Lighting

Can lights are hard to avoid and can be essential to completing tasks. While I do not care for the holes in the ceiling that recessed lighting requires, this type of light source can be useful in the kitchen. Next comes the decorative lighting. It's common to choose pendants to hang over an island, but I let the shape of the island dictate my fixture choice.

Cabinet Hardware

Hardware is your opportunity to play with finishes and styles. It will function the same way regardless. I approach finishes in a kitchen with a mixed metal attitude. When everything from the plumbing to the cabinet hardware is of the same

If cooking is a passion, cookbooks should be visible so they can be enjoyed. When designing a kitchen, dedicate an area for books early in the process.

Solid color accents, such as the island and chair cushions here, work beautifully in clean, bright, all-white kitchens.

There are two schools of thought when it comes to a kitchen island. Some folks like a look where everything blends. I, on the other hand, am always identifying opportunities for another color, pattern, or surface. Especially in a monotone kitchen, think about how a soft blue or intense dark green would offer a distinct contrast and interest. If a new paint color doesn't work for you, maybe try a different texture of wood. Think about beadboard or a stained wood base that highlights the wood grain. The base of an island is below your sight line, so it's nothing that you will ever be looking at directly. Unless of course, someone knocks over their cereal bowl, and for that I have no solutions, except that I can remember being on the floor a time or twenty wiping up spilled something. Luckily, those days are long in the rear-view mirror for me.

BEAUTY BOOST

In the kitchen, think big when it comes to accessories for the island and countertops. A collection of vases in mismatched sizes and colors should be corralled on a tray. Another option is to place one large vessel on the island that accommodates something tall, like branches. They will last longer than cut flowers. Decorative platters or trays propped against a backsplash add dimension and personality, especially when they've been used and show a patina of dings and dents.

ABOVE *The base of a kitchen island is an ideal place to introduce a secondary color: Because it's below eye level, its presence is subtle.*

OPPOSITE *Function can come in many sizes, from the large proportions of an entire room to diminutive moments such as a bar cart that can be organized with everything needed for drinks with friends and family.*

metal, there's a strong chance that your kitchen will feel dated sooner.

BATHROOMS

Bathrooms may be smaller than kitchens, but that doesn't necessarily mean that they are small. Do you want your bathroom to serve only for personal care, or will you use it to dress in, too?

Vanities and Countertops

Since I personally gravitate toward some color, I look at bathrooms as a place where you can make a commitment to it in a relatively small way. Plus, since vanity cabinets are far below eye level, the color won't be glaring at you, but rather will lend a spirited moment of joy. When it comes to the vanity mirror, opt for one that is beautifully framed. Even if sheet mirror covers the wall, installing a decorative mirror over a sheet mirror will show your ability to create layers and interest.

Furniture in the Bathroom

If there is room for seating in your bathroom, it will check a couple of boxes. Not only does seating provide a spot to put on hosiery or shoes, it will be another spot to add fabric and soften the hard edges of glass, tile, and cabinetry. Traditionalists tend to love a French- or Swedish-style chair in this room. For those who are attracted to clean, modern lines, a sleek armless chair in an indoor-outdoor printed fabric might do the trick. In the case of bathroom seating, the requirements are comfort and scale. After that, choose what fits your style.

Beauty Boost

Take advantage of the soft spots in a bathroom. Monogram your towels, and add an appliqué trim that will coordinate with the room's palette. Contain cotton balls and swabs in decorative canisters of your liking. In bathrooms for my guests, I like to add a small flower arrangement and display hand cream and soap in pretty pumps.

ABOVE *A classic mirrored wall over the vanity becomes intriguing when it's edged with a gold frame and topped with a lighting fixture. There's always an opportunity to elevate basics.*

OPPOSITE *A soaking tub encourages relaxing and resting. Make the experience even more enjoyable by hanging a piece of artwork on the wall above it.*

TOP *Consciously leaving open space in places like this medicine cabinet allows all the contents to be visible and minimizes duplicate purchases of the same product.*

BOTTOM *In a shower space, tile with an invigorating pattern delivers a fresh aesthetic.*

OPPOSITE *A place to activate beauty calls for pretty seating. Picking a fabric that you love for a vanity stool makes the experience of getting ready for the day or an event extra glamorous.*

ABOVE *Consistency is important for design. In a bathroom, when a tile treatment adds a joyful vibe to the walls, I continue it on the floor, too.*

OPPOSITE *Old-school tile can give a fresh kick when you use a sharp, bright color to contrast with white. Here, apple green and fuchsia make a strong case for color.*

Small touches such as this elevate the guests' experiences to make them feel special.

CLOSETS AND DRESSING ROOMS

We all likely have some investment in the contents of our closet, so it only makes sense that a closet, dressing room, and laundry room, for that matter, are useful, well thought out, and are given the same attention to detail as our bedrooms and living areas. After all, it's where our garments will be laundered, organized, and stored. Before you carve out significant space in your home to style a photo-ready dressing room or closet, consider the following:

• How do you want this space to look? Are you the type that flourishes in surroundings that are highly decorated with colors and patterns, or is your fashion creativity clearer to you in an environment that is left simple and clean?

• What does your wardrobe look like? Do you have a diverse wardrobe with clothing for many situations, from business meetings and lunches with friends to cocktail parties and formal affairs, athletic events, golf outings, and that occasional situation that calls for a cowboy hat and boots? Or do you adhere to the pared-down capsule method way of dress, buying key pieces in smart neutrals that can be mixed and glamorized with accessories?

Consider your accessory inventory so storage can be divided effectively. Are you a minimalist or a collector? Borrow upgrade ideas from the kitchen and set shoes on pull-out shelves with door fronts if you want to conceal them instead of displaying them on stationary shelves. Choose acrylic shelf dividers that will allow you to file clutches like upright envelopes. For ties, belts, and jewelry, invest in drawer inserts that will keep everything neat and divided.

Beauty Boost

In the closet, you don't have to look far to hit your decorative peak. Display the fashion itself. Hang a row of silk scarves on hooks for vibrant color. Display handbags prominently on a shelf.

ABOVE *Highlight closet doors with a fresh paint color to make them as fashionable as the garments and accessories within.*

OPPOSITE *An organized closet—and organized accessories, in particular—make getting dressed a pleasure.*

A clothes closet or dressing room is not complete without at least one mirror. Full-length is best to assess the full scope of your ensemble.

LAUNDRY ROOMS

Laundry rooms today are in their best shape ever, and offer much more than laundry care. You might assess what you want your laundry room to be if you need a redo.

- What functions does the room need to address?

- Do you plan to do other activities, such as crafts or computer work, there?
- Will the space be shared with the family pets?

There are many ways to configure laundry rooms so that you can efficiently care for garments plus do a whole lot more there.

Beauty Boost

Decant laundry powders, detergents, and pods into clear-lidded jars. Remember those bowls and trays from your flea market strolls? Use them

ABOVE *Black and white can look strict and graphic. Folding playful motifs into its scheme can soften the look of a laundry room to make it not only functional, but stylish, too.*

TOP *Invest in attractive matching boxes and bins to organize anything that needs to be at the ready before you walk out the door.*

BOTTOM *Even if it has small proportions, a laundry room can be multipurpose. If there's room, consider installing a refrigerator to have a variety of drinks available to take on the go.*

OPPOSITE *Functional rooms can be cheerful, too, with the right mix of patterns. Here, the mudroom enjoys a double dose of the floral wallpaper and the striped floor through mirrored paneling on doors.*

for loose change and other finds in pockets that shouldn't make their way through the wash cycle.

ORGANIZING AESTHETICS: KEEPING THINGS NEAT

Orderly design, in addition to its visual appeal, comes with a sense of calm. Having a place for everything and everything in its place is the start to success.

Knowing where contents are located and adhering to putting them back where they belong eliminates chaos. So does the routine of decluttering. When we rid ourselves of excess, our minds are free to focus.

The good news: There are ample choices out there for devising systems to create a tidy setup. Browse the aisles of your local storage and container stores and analyze what is offered. If you want your contents to be stored in a uniform manner—an ideal approach for kitchens, pantries, and garages—opt for clear containers so you can see what you have and what you don't. I find myself choosing containers with lids, whether the contents need it or not, so they can be stacked. Something that I've also learned over the years is to use square and rectangular containers. They allow me to utilize every inch of shelf and drawer area, where circular shapes would waste some real estate.

For rooms with my personal things, my organizing accoutrements tend to represent my style. For instance, I collect vintage hotel ashtrays. These are perfect to corral jewelry in my bedroom. Similarly, bowls are ideal to hold binder clips and stamps in an office. I also think it's chic and interesting to use a vintage tray to keep a handful business cards accessible on a desk.

I never suggest buying for the sake of buying, but having the following in your decorative vault will give structure to storing these common items:

- **Bowls.** Ideal for little bits that could easily roll away or get pushed off a surface. Jewelry, keys, small office supplies, and coins belong in little bowls.

- **Boxes.** Lidded boxes have so many purposes, but for me they are a problem solver in the family room or anywhere there's a television. Place remotes there, *all* of them. Here's another little trick that has saved my family on too many occasions to count. Put passwords for the modem and streaming services on a

Knowing where contents are located and adhering to putting them back where they belong eliminates chaos.

card (so everyone has access), and store it in the box with the remotes. If you ever become logged out—and I know that it's happened to you, too—the passwords will be handy. We all know the frustration of having to reset a password when you're settling in to watch your favorite show.

- **Trays.** Have a couple on hand, with and without handles. Small trays can be used the same way small bowls can. Large trays can organize stacks of books on a cocktail table or console table.

Functional spaces were once intentionally void of joyful design because nobody considered the tasks performed to be joyful. Reality reminds us, however, that we can't avoid certain responsibilities, and that they can be pleasant and rewarding when executed in an inspired environment. When the surroundings work well and are organized, you have the perfect recipe for being productive.

chapter 7

JOYFUL ROOMS

OPPOSITE AND ABOVE *If color is what makes you happy, go one step further with patterns in loose, jovial geometrics.*

PAGE 212 *Choose a palette of lively patterns and colors for spaces you want to revive and inspire.*

*I*t's no secret that what we *observe* is what leads our passion for style within our homes. We tend to gravitate toward all things visual to help unveil our own style, which in the end awaits approval from our own two eyes. I believe in designing spaces that are inherently joyful and don't take themselves too seriously. Such a setting is often the backdrop for life's happiest moments, whether it's a front hall that makes you smile when you get home or a glowing room in which to enjoy a cocktail at the end of the day.

We scroll through imagery, rifle through wallpaper samples, run our fingers over textiles, inspect furniture's wood grain, dream of color schemes, connect with artwork, and amass personal treasures, all with the same goal in mind—to translate what we perceive as beauty into our own vocabulary, then into our homes to encourage a gracious and lovely environment. The aesthetic, however, is only one aspect of design. Even more important is the *feeling* that emanates from our creations, and the one feeling I hope they evoke above all others is that of *joy*.

We blast lively patterns and colors into spaces when we want to revive and inspire. We mix textures when we want to be content and wrapped in comfort. We provide a variety of seating possibilities in our kitchens, which we know will become hubs for frenzy and life's social occasions. Regardless of the type of room, each space should not only dazzle with its decoration, but emote an energy that brings us happiness and a feeling of well-being.

A beautiful room without joy is simply a collection of things. However, when its visual charm delivers a smile, too, then a space is personal and

ABOVE *Small flourishes can yield a big impact. I'm known for adding monograms, particularly to linens, for a personal touch at the table.*

OPPOSITE *A quartet of coordinating paintings by one artist confidently establishes a palette of bright hues in abstract florals.*

it's *yours.* As you immerse yourself in this final chapter, I hope that you consider your own specific favorites and preferences and think about ways that you can shine a light on them. Whether you're using the prettiest chinoiserie print, an antique rug with a perfect patina, or a piece crafted by an artisan from your recent travel destination, your biggest design asset is the mood you create.

DEFINING JOY

Joy is a very personal emotion, and what makes it resonate is not the same for everyone. Visually, it could mean the use of a favorite color, perhaps an intense turquoise that reminds you of the tropical water near a favorite beach destination or a forest green that evokes the pine trees dotting a mountaintop when you breeze by during ski trips. On the other hand, a joyful space can be void of color entirely, a calming respite that provides serenity and relaxation after a long day or night. In my home, for instance, joy comes from our light-flooded sun-room, where a wall of windows encourages a glance into to my garden, where my beloved Jack Russell terriers frolic. Joy could come from an heirloom chair that hugs us with memories of a grandparent. I regularly wear an especially meaningful charm on a chain, a golden clover. My engraved initials, along with those of my husband and two sons, embellish one side, and initials of my grandparents and their children (my mother, aunt, and uncle) are on the other. The medallion once dangled from my grandmother's charm bracelet and now, in a way, my family is nearby even if we are all scattered in different places. I glance down at it on its long chain, and that tactile presence of my loved ones around my neck always makes me happy and brings me solace. Even though the origins of joy are different for all of us, the results are similar. We want moments in life that will make us smile and imbue us with a lighthearted sense of place and gratitude.

ABOVE *Some palettes are popular and perennial, but seek out the unexpected. This unusual mix of purples, blues, and butternut yellow is new and fresh.*

OPPOSITE *Ceramic lamps, a raffia console table, and a malachite mirror frame demonstrate that there is no need to be shy when mixing materials. An airy floral on the wall behind adds energy and movement.*

Bold color always makes a room a showstopper. In this case, otherwise neutral furnishings are highlighted by fuchsia walls.

Aquas and soft greens visually cool the environment—ideal for spaces that are near the water.

Joy doesn't have to live on a large scale. Take advantage of window seats. They invite natural light to pour through and welcome cheerful colors and novelty motifs.

Happy moments can be contained in a small vignette. Here, a bedside table painted in a creamy teal, contrasted with doors clad in caning, lends just enough interest.

When you are establishing a theme, consider every surface of the room. This trellis, semiflush light fixture reflects the delicacy of the nursery's design.

HOW TO ACHIEVE A JOYFUL ROOM

Joyful rooms stream from two channels of creativity. They can be the final emotion that's the result of your meaningful objects. Although I enjoy the process of creating the space, the biggest excitement to me is when I witness the exuberance and jubilation of homeowners after an installation. When my team reveals a home to its owners, and they walk into their recently installed space for the first time, I know that at that moment they will understand that the sum of the design components is far greater than its parts. Sometimes it can be challenging for people to see how each element will play with the next or how an outlier such as an accent color or novelty piece of furniture will work with what's already there. I find this challenge especially true in a large area such as a living room or kitchen, where there are so many considerations and activities to accommodate. However, once architectural details are established and all the furnishings are placed, the overall scheme oftentimes satisfies with alluring aesthetics and an easy flow and function. That pairing of form and function is sure to sound a happy note.

Second, and on the flip side, there are some rooms, or parts of rooms, that are intended solely for the purpose of pleasure. Keep in mind that these environments don't need to function per se, but are designed for enjoyment. The scale of

The biggest excitement to me is when I witness the exuberance and jubilation of homeowners after an installation.

such a space varies; it can be an overall room or a wow-moment vignette within a larger space. Think about children's rooms, craft rooms and workspaces, powder rooms, and dressing rooms. These rooms are likely not grand in proportion, but are great in their abilities to delight. Next, I will break down a few of these rooms specifically,

Nurseries are the perfect place for sweet color palettes that might be too juvenile for other parts of the house.

ABOVE LEFT AND OPPOSITE *For a multicolored backdrop, choose a piece of furniture to highlight one of the hues. Here, a sunny yellow dresser extends the cheerful outlook of the scheme.*

ABOVE RIGHT *An abstract dot pattern covers a classic armchair.*

to offer ideas on how to charm with details so that these spaces are blissful, not in disarray or merely an afterthought.

CHILDREN'S ROOMS

There is often a poignant emotion that accompanies thinking back on our childhood bedrooms. Aside from sparking memories of play dates, bed-

time reading, and studying at our desks, there is another reason for that. Childhood comes with unbridled creativity. When we are young, we are not trapped by design rules, function considerations, coordinating expected colors, or anything else. Our top priority as children is to be happy, and our imaginations have complete freedom, so when we beg our parents for an update using the color that we just identified as our favorite for a

Children's rooms should spark imagination. Mix patterns both small and oversized, and highlight nooks in a charming, sassy color.

A piece of furniture in a hip color puts an
exclamation mark on a room's palette—in this case,
a shelving unit pops in a bright accent hue.

ABOVE *In a child's room, choose a novelty that doesn't take design too seriously. Here, a chair with a sports team logo hints at fandom without being too loud.*

ABOVE *Artwork satisfies a lot of wishes. Find a subject that your child loves and use it in multiples for a fun display.*

OPPOSITE *In a room with lots of other whimsical moments, the ceiling's bold but basic stripe draws attention without being fussy.*

ABOVE *Playing with patterns and colors like the blues, greens, and natural materials on this mood board can assist in understanding scale and where texture is helpful.*

ABOVE *Blue and white is charming, nostalgic, and versatile. If traditional cobalt is not to your liking, try blue in a shade that does resonate with you. Introduce textures such as smooth art glass or glazed ceramics.*

OPPOSITE *Part of layering is enhancing certain elements and tempering others. Aqua is toned down by peeking through lattice that caps the walls and ceiling. Toss pillows and ceramic stools heighten the intensity of the color.*

school project, or suggest building a loft so we can sleep at an elevated height, we know that if our wishes are met, joyful days are ahead. That's a child's perspective.

POWDER ROOMS

The biggest asset of a powder room is its diminutive proportions. Whatever design you choose to imbue this tiny space with will be contained, so my advice is to go for it. Chances are, you've turned your head on more than one occasion when you have spotted large-scale, patterned statement wallpapers. They are dramatic and can't help but make an impression. I'm rarely shy designing a powder room. It's an opportunity to go bold and use a pattern or strong color scheme that might not be practical or palatable in large doses. Cost is another reward for choosing a statement pattern in a powder room. In a large room, having enough rolls of a covering to blanket the walls, or enough yards of fabric to make floor-length window panels, can be rather costly. Making a splash in a powder room, however, probably doesn't require a large amount of material, and thus you can achieve something special on a reasonable budget.

Don't forget the ceiling. It's an ideal opportunity to show off your contrast skills. For example, if you've applied a large-scale chinoiserie pattern to the walls, consider a coordinating woven wallcovering such as grass cloth or raffia for texture for the ceiling. You can always go the opposite way, too. I'm drawn to a ceiling with a little reflective sparkle, such as gold or silver leaf, to create an elegant and glamorous atmosphere. A lacquered ceiling with a high-gloss finish also elevates the glow factor. Most people aren't in the powder room for very long, which means there is little chance of tiring of it. This space is where daring design incubates and comes to fruition, so in your own home make the powder room the jewel box that proves that big things do come in small packages.

ABOVE *If you want to give a room personality, there's no better way than a chic mix of patterns: Create a masculine vibe with seating in a powerful color, such as this wicker chair (that nods to the shape of a baseball glove) with red cushions.*

OPPOSITE *Assign every family member their own color for an organized space that is also artful.*

WORKSPACES

Workspaces have never been better looking or more accommodating than they are today. When I say "workspaces," I'm not necessarily referring to spaces at our jobs, although they can be spaces for that, too. *Workspace* can also mean a place for household management, administrative tasks such as bill-paying and scheduling. Workspaces also include the laundry; a craft room where gifts are wrapped throughout the year; and the spot where you channel your own artistic spirit with painting, potting, or whatever your hobbies and chosen activities are.

An environment can be inspirational when it was created with thought about its decoration. On the other hand, when an environment lacks personality, it can paralyze the creative spirit. It is always important to consider the appearance of every room within your home. A room doesn't have to be formal, and it should encourage energy and life. Here are some of the ways I make workspaces individualized.

ORGANIZATION WITH STYLE

One component that helps a workspace function is organization. I'll admit to the following if *you* will, because I know that it happens to all of us. On occasion, I've spent plenty of time organizing pantries, closets, and offices and rethinking every nook and cranny that's assigned to specific contents. When disorganization exists, so can underlying and unnecessary chaos and stress. When everything is just so, it saves the time used for searching for what you need, and that is sure to bring you a joyful experience.

Organization is not solely about the function, though. Your craft room, for instance, may already be equipped with containers for supplies. Are they coordinated and uniform or an assembly of mismatched boxes, containers, and jars that keep things tidy but don't necessarily *look* tidy? If the latter describes your situation, consider switching them out for matching containers.

Spending time outdoors on a bluebird day lightens the mood. Creating an environment that enhances the surroundings makes the experience all the more enjoyable. Furniture with comfortable cushions ensures that guests will linger.

When the vibe is lively, happiness is never far behind. An assembly of geometrics, florals, and abstracts dances with varying motifs within a symmetrical furniture arrangement.

Using a label maker adds another layer of function and design. Pick an interesting font to add personality to the labels.

THE GREAT OUTDOORS

Your outdoor spaces are inherently feel-good areas. After all, if you are spending time outside, it's probably to absorb the lovely breezes, bright rays of sunshine, and an array of greenery in the fresh air. How inviting the outdoors is on a nice day affects whether you sit in the shade with your book or plunge into the pool. Time outdoors also may reveal that a crisp but refreshing chill in the air requires a sweater and a long stick to roast marshmallows over a crackling firepit.

Your natural surroundings may provide plenty of pleasure already. They can be enhanced further, though, by well-considered hardscaping to define outdoor rooms that have similar visual comforts to those of their interior cousins. Ensure that furniture has inviting cushions. You will find yourself spending more time in your outdoor space if you can relax for longer stretches. Comfort matters during lengthy stays outside for an extra hit of vitamin D, for example. Adorn seating with throw pillows and throw blankets in festive colors that aren't necessarily the mainstays of nature. You might coordinate planters so that they, too, support your style. On that same note, fine-tune your landscape artistry by thinking about the colors and textures that will grow from flowers and other plants. If you plan on dining al fresco, consider a suite of outdoor-friendly melamine or metal dishes so you can fashion a coordinated tablescape that charms. Some dishes are now available in beautiful patterns that imitate those of fine porcelain. The same is true of napkins. Think about a delicate floral, toile, or striped napkin for occasions during summer months, and a plaid for fall gatherings where pumpkins might dance down the table's center for the season.

TOP *Furniture with similar flair to interior pieces manages to season outdoor spaces with style.*

BOTTOM *Stately flowers deserve cachepots of equal style. A chinoiserie bowl, vase, and ginger jar have enough visual weight to display orchids and branches.*

OPPOSITE *A blue-and-white foundation is ideal because it works with so many other colors. Use it in a space such as a light-flooded breakfast nook, where you'll want to start each day with fresh blooms from the garden or the market.*

Dining outside on a sunny day sets a tone of joy before the meal is even served. Add pattern with a tablecloth that will blissfully complement the flower gardens that surround the space.

Simple placement of a pair of chairs like the green Adirondack ones here provide all that is needed for an afternoon chat, with iced tea or lemonade.

A JOYFUL FINISH:
THE IMPORTANCE OF FLOWERS

Above all other design elements in interiors, there is one that is no-fail when it comes to creating joy. That element is flowers.

We all have so many options for picking up different varieties of flowers: fresh and preserved, plants, and ornamental grasses. When you buy the flowers yourself, chances are they will be in the colors and types that you love, but even when they are sent to you and are not to your aesthetic preference, remember there is joy in the fact that someone thought of you. I often rearrange a bouquet by plucking out some of the filler greens and moving the colors that aren't my favorites to a vase from my own collection for a look that works for me.

Containers for Flowers

To display flowers, first consider the container that holds them. I've built my inventory of flower containers from sources including pieces we have had since our wedding, vintage shops and estate sales, and the shelves at some favorite big-box home stores. I own a handful of special silver and crystal vases, but from a design perspective, I'm particularly drawn to silhouettes over materials. As you are out and about, my advice is to look for interesting forms. This is one area of design that can deliver big impact for nominal prices, so if your budget presents some challenges and constraints, lean on flower containers to show your styling skills. For instance, you might start looking for ivory-colored vases, or any color that you like. Commit to a color and begin your search. Also consider using found pieces from your own home. I love putting a small bouquet into one of my children's silver baby cups, which I have kept in my cabinet for many years. I also love to put plants such as ferns in vintage wicker wastebaskets. Find a space at home to store your collections of cachepots, vases, and clown containers so they are accessible on a regular basis. I often save colorful glass

ABOVE *Repetition is your exclamation point in design. Multiples of glass vases and rattan ones emphasize their ability to work together.*

OPPOSITE *Choose accessories that will read clearly through different glass styles. The leaded glass windows on this door required something bold and colorful like jadeite to make a statement.*

Baskets are optimal for garden heavyweights.

ABOVE *An unexpected mix of tableware is bound to make guests smile. A vintage cabbage plate tops formal English bone china, which rests on a natural fiber place mat and an overscale ikat cloth.*

OPPOSITE *A gathering with friends and family around the table offers joy because of the people there. Add an extra spark of bliss with a layered table scheme full of color, contrast, and varying materials.*

candle containers, which can be perfect for a mid-sized flower arrangement. You will eventually amass enough for a table centerpiece and can add a compact bouquet of mini roses or herbs to them.

I don't often put flowers in clear, utilitarian vases. They serve their purpose for flowers that we send and receive via a local florist, but they don't suggest anything about personal style or the aesthetics of our home. A crystal vase is a different case, however. Crystal vases tend to have classic silhouettes, and if they are cut glass, the facets reflect light and add sparkle to flowers.

Colored glass vases deliver a fashionable statement. Build an assortment of colored glass vases in the same color or same color family. Imagine the stunning presence of simple white roses or hydrangeas displayed in a gradation of pink glass vases. If you are aiming for a slightly country and casual vibe, think about pairing turquoise-colored canning jars with daisies.

Baskets are optimal for garden heavyweights. For instance, I find marigolds, black-eyed Susans, and geraniums charming when potted in baskets. If you use a basket, make sure there is a glass or plastic liner inside to contain the water.

Hydrangeas and peonies are beloved because of their volume and impact. I like to show them off in ivory-colored ceramic pitchers or spongeware pitchers in late summer.

For a streamlined look, containers in black or brown are your best bet. Somehow, I often find myself choosing a black container when I want to make a graphic statement with only a single bloom. Containers in masculine shades can also enhance rough materials such as branches or ornamental grasses. They can also amplify the deep tones of red roses, aubergine-colored calla lilies, or ornamental cabbages.

While the aesthetics of a space are significant, they certainly aren't everything. Joy doesn't have to be created by visuals, but by the people who are in a room and the activity that transpires there. Most important, though, create architectural and decorative interiors that encourage joy to radiate from *you*.

Joy in design means encouraging a smile with elements that don't take life too seriously. Whether in a space for kids or adults, add a playful note.

Acknowledgments

I acknowledge with an abundance of gratitude:

• Mike, my husband, my Sweetie, my partner, who has both impatiently and patiently stuck by me through the uncharted territory of creating a book.

• Henry and George, my darling sons, who folded fabrics and assisted in my design library before I had interns.

• Ed Madden, my incredible stepfather, who treats me like his own daughter. Ed prioritizes his family above all else and has been a constant support and great encourager.

• My ARI family (my staff). You are the ones who truly make it happen. Hannah Jacobus, Sara Kent-Schneider, and Emma Bingham, your constant dedication, attention to detail, and eagerness to learn make working with you all a gift.

• Ellie Cullman, whom I was privileged to work for and learn from. Ellie is the epitome of grace and leads by example not only as a designer, but with her thoughtful, generous, and inclusive approach. I am ever grateful to Ellie for imparting the invaluable knowledge of decorating and design details that I carry with me to this day.

• Jill Waage, Sophie Donelson, Amy Panos, Monika Eyers, Jessica Thomas, and all of the magazine editors who have shared my work in their publications.

• Krissa Rossbund, who has given my work a platform and place to be seen and helped shape the voice of this book.

• Dara Caponigro and the whole Schumacher team, for the beautiful prints that grace the cover and endpapers of this book.

• Liz Lidgett, for helping find the perfect pieces for our clients and loaning me artwork for photo shoots whenever needed.

• Sara Bliss Hamblett, a friend for thirty years and a brilliant writer, who helped me distill and shape my design philosophies and images into comprehensible chapters.

• Stephen Orr, who became a fast and forever friend. Thank you for your advice and stories and for kindly writing such a lovely foreword.

• My incredible clients, who entrust me to be a good steward of their homes and became great friends along the way. I have grown and learned from you all during each and every project.

• Alison Fargis and Stonesong, for steering my ship in the right direction and keeping it on course.

• Shawna Mullen and the Abrams team who made my vision a reality.

• Adam Albright, Rick Lozier, David Tsay, John Bessler, Carmel Brantley, Thomas Loof, Paige Peterson Connolly, and Kim Cornelison for all the breathtaking images in this book.

• The talented and incredible fine artists, whose artwork improves the homes and lives of our clients.

• Marisa Marcantonio, my darling, cheerleading sister.

• Cathy, Billy, Danielle, the Malteasers, and all of my DLN friends, for so much incredible design travel, camaraderie, get-togethers, and shoptalk.

• The Design Leadership Network. This organization has opened so many doors and has been a huge part of my growing ARI.

• Miss Porter's School and Trinity College, for giving me so much more than an education.

• Our Onteora community, especially the women: Andrea, Tracy, Jennifer, Jenny, Gillian, Abby C., Abby S., Betsy, Ginny, Seldy, and Karen.

• Deborah Goodrich Royce, for always being kind and encouraging as a fellow author.

• Parker and Minnie, for all the cuddles, licks, and naps by my side while I worked on this book.

About the Author

Amanda Reynal began her interior design career at Cullman & Kravis in New York. At the firm, she learned to design interiors filled with exceptional customized detail coupled with fine art and antiques.

She graduated from Miss Porter's School and then received a BA in art history from Trinity College before studying at New York School of Interior Design. Her education was critical in influencing her love of aesthetics, art, and architecture.

In 2001, Amanda left Manhattan to further develop her signature style and launch her own design business studio in Des Moines, Iowa.

She later opened a sunny studio and home shop. She also spent time in London, studying European decorative arts and architecture. Amanda's sought-after aesthetic is at once eye-catching, sophisticated, and accessible. Her work has been featured in *House Beautiful*, *Traditional Home*, *Better Homes & Gardens*, *Elle Decor*, and the *New York Times*. She is known for designing joyful spaces that highlight color, art, and playful details. She is dedicated to bringing a fresh and current approach to every project; her work is grounded in traditional design concepts, but always with an updated kick.

@amandareynalinteriors

Editor: Shawna Mullen
Designer: Darilyn Lowe Carnes with Anna Christian
Managing Editor: Annalea Manalili
Production Manager: Denise LaCongo

Library of Congress Control Number: 2023930349

ISBN: 978-1-4197-6566-7
eISBN: 978-1-64700-883-3

Text copyright © 2023 Amanda Reynal

Cover © 2023 Abrams
Endpapers: "Bouquet Toss," fabric and wallpaper by
Celerie Kemble for Schumacher

Printed and bound in China
10 9 8 7 6 5 4 3 2 1

Abrams books are available at special discounts when
purchased in quantity for premiums and promotions as
well as fundraising or educational use. Special editions
can also be created to specification. For details, contact
specialsales@abramsbooks.com or the address below.

Abrams® is a registered trademark of
Harry N. Abrams, Inc.

ABRAMS The Art of Books
195 Broadway, New York, NY 10007
abramsbooks.com

All photos by Adam Albright except:

Pages 4, 102–103, 124, 214 by Carmel Brantley
Pages 8, 23, 66, 71, 75, 128, 136–137, 152–153,
      154–155, 162, 175, 176, 242–243, 244–245 by
      Thomas Loof
Page 19 by John Bessler
Pages 24–25, 26, 32, 38, 40, 41, 54, 63, 70, 80–81, 90
      (bottom), 98–99, 100 (right), 109, 141, 160–161,
      166, 168–169, 181, 199, 220–221, 223, 230, 232
      (right), 235 by Rick Lozier
Pages 44, 108, 146, 159, 180, 214 by Paige Peterson
      Photography
Page 74 by Alana Harris
Pages 92, 93, 94–95, 233, 241 by David Tsay
Page 184 by Kim Cornelison
Pages 246, 248–249 by Marty Baldwin